Life with Lacan

Life with Lacan

Catherine Millot

Translated by Andrew Brown

polity

First published in French as *La vie avec Lacan* © Éditions Gallimard, 2016

This English translation © Polity Press, 2018

This paperback edition © Polity Press, 2025

Polity Press
65 Bridge Street
Cambridge CB2 1UR, UK

Polity Press
111 River Street
Hoboken, NJ 07030, USA

ISBN-13: 978-1-5095-2501-0
ISBN-13: 978-1-5095-2502-7 (pb)

Library of Congress Cataloging-in-Publication Data

Names: Millot, Catherine, author.
Title: Life with Lacan / Catherine Millot.
Other titles: Vie avec Lacan. English
Description: English edition. | Medford, MA : Polity, 2018. | Includes bibliographical references and index.
Identifiers: LCCN 2017036535 (print) | LCCN 2017047063 (ebook) | ISBN 9781509525058 (Epub) | ISBN 9781509525010 (hardback)
Subjects: LCSH: Lacan, Jacques, 1901-1981. | Millot, Catherine. | Psychoanalysts--France--Biography. | Authors, French--20th century--Biography. | Authors, French--21st century--Biography.
Classification: LCC BF109.L28 (ebook) | LCC BF109.L28 M553 2018 (print) | DDC 150.19/5092 [B] --dc23
LC record available at https://lccn.loc.gov/2017036535

A catalogue record for this book is available from the British Library.

Typeset in 12.5 on 15 pt Adobe Garamond by
Servis Filmsetting Ltd, Stockport, Cheshire
Printed and bound by CPI Group (UK) Ltd, Croydon, CR0 4YY

For further information on Polity, visit our website:
politybooks.com

There was a time when I felt that I had grasped Lacan's essential being from within – that I had gained, as it were, a close sense of his relation to the world, a mysterious access to that intimate place from which sprang his relation to people and things, and even to himself. It was as if I had slipped inside him.

This feeling of grasping him from the inside was accompanied by the impression that I myself was comprehended, in the sense of being completely included within his own understanding, which extended far beyond my ken. His mind – with its breadth and depth – his mental world, enclosed mine in the way a bigger sphere contains a smaller one. I came across a similar idea in the letter where Madame Teste talks about her husband.[1] Just as she felt transparent to her

[1] Translator's note: French writer Paul Valéry's character Monsieur Teste ('Mister Head') is a highly intellectual and rarefied figure.

husband, I felt transparent to Lacan, convinced that he had an absolute knowledge of me. I had nothing to hide, no mystery to keep from him: this gave me complete freedom with him. But it went further than that. An essential part of my being was vouchsafed to him; he would watch over it, I was relieved of it. I lived at his side for years, in this state of lightness.

One day, however, he was busy manipulating those rings of string that were such a knotty problem for him, when he abruptly told me: 'See that? It's you!' Like anyone, like any random person, I was the real that escaped his grasp and that gave him such a headache. I was overwhelmed by a sudden feeling of respect for what within me resisted him, in the way that the real alone resists.

When I say 'his being', what do I mean? His particularity, his singularity, what in him was irreducible, the weight of his reality. When I now try to grasp his being anew, it's his power of concentration that I recall, his almost permanent concentration on the object that he was thinking of and that he never let go. In the end, he had simplified himself to an extreme degree. In one sense, that was all he now was: a pure concentration that merged with his desire, and made this desire tangible.

I recognized this concentration in the way he walked, headfirst, as if borne along by his weight, catching his balance in every step he took. But this very instability gave one a sense of his determination, he would never deviate an inch from his route, he would keep right on to the end, always moving straight ahead, without paying any attention to what might get in his way – he seemed to ignore such obstacles (which in any case were beneath his contempt). He liked to remind people that his star sign was Aries, the Ram.

The first time I saw him walking was on the paths of the Cinque Terre in Italy, where, after lunch, in the lazy summer heat – it was August – he would drag his entourage after him. They did not dare protest. He marched on ahead, with grim determination. The risks of sunstroke for himself or the rest were of no account. So we walked on, from one coastal village to the next, across the hills overlooking the sea, returning in the little local train.

That summer, he went water skiing in the narrow bay of Manarola. Firmly gripping the waterski handle, and without ever leaving the boat's wake, here too he went straight ahead. The following winter, on the slopes of the Tignes ski resort, the only manoeuvre he seemed to know was the schuss. This had led to him breaking a leg a few years earlier. That was the time when Gloria, his secretary, had started to work for him. Being immobilized put him in a furious temper; he was like a bear with a sore head, and he took it out on the poor woman, who lost patience with him. He was lying stretched out on his bed, his leg in plaster; she grabbed hold of his leg, lifted it up and then suddenly dropped it. Taken aback by this woman's refusal to be intimidated, Lacan immediately changed his tone and suddenly took an interest in her, asking her questions about where she was from and her whole life story. That day, a bond of unshakeable loyalty was forged between them.

Later on, I would often go with him from his country house in Guitrancourt to the golf course in which he held shares, though he never actually played. The golf course was just a destination for his walks. But 'walks' isn't really the word. Here again, he would march straight off, his head lowered, through woods and fields, getting entangled in the thickets or bogged down in the greasy clods of freshly ploughed earth, never straying from his route. Indeed, I wondered how he knew which way to go, but he never got lost. I would follow along in my wellies, while he unconcernedly got his elegant, custom-made shoes covered in mud. Once he had reached the golf course, he would phone Jesus, his caretaker at Guitrancourt – his 'kindly Jesus' as he liked to call him – asking him to come and take us home in his car.

It was just the same when he drove: his head forward, gripping the steering wheel, treating obstacles with contempt, as one of my women friends noted, never slowing down even for a red light – and as for observing the right of way … well, let's not go there. The first time, on the autoroute, travelling at some 120 mph, I had a fit of the giggles which I suppressed only with difficulty. But even if I'd burst out laughing, he'd never have noticed; he was concentrating too hard.

One day, however, he was forced to slam the brakes on so as not to crash into the car ahead of us which had suddenly slowed down. But braking wasn't his forte; the car skidded, and that put an end to the sense of invulnerability that had filled me when I was at his side. I started to feel scared, and it was torture to travel as his passenger. There was no point in imploring him to slow down. Once, his stepdaughter Laurence had come up with a bright idea: she asked him to drive more slowly so that she could 'look at the countryside'. He told her: 'Just pay more attention'.

Only once, in my company, was he stopped by the police on the autoroute as he drove back from Guitrancourt. On Sunday evenings, when the traffic was always heavy, he was used to driving on the hard shoulder and overtaking the line of cars stuck in the queue, whose drivers grew furious at being overtaken on the right and would suddenly swing their cars out into his path even though this risked causing a collision. That evening we were taken to the police station near the Saint-Cloud tunnel, where he had to wait a long time before he could argue that a medical emergency had justified this offence. He showed no sign of impatience while awaiting his turn to be questioned. Sometimes, the real can assume the face of the police.

His way of driving was part and parcel of his ethics. It is no coincidence that, as a parable, he told the following story to his analyst Rudolph

Loewenstein, a heavyweight in the International Psychoanalytical Association. Once, he'd been in a tunnel, driving his little car, when he saw a lorry overtaking another vehicle and heading towards him. He continued to step on the gas, and forced the lorry driver to back down. It was like a show of strength, but the message, rather, was that he couldn't be intimidated and would never give way to force.

He told me this story at a time when he still liked talking about himself. He also related a recent incident that had left him feeling bitter. Two crooks had burst into his consulting room around 7 pm, pushing aside Paquita who opened the door once Gloria had left work at the end of the afternoon. They'd come into his office, where he was with Moustafa Safouan who was being supervised by him. The thugs told him they wanted his money, and pointed a revolver at him. He told them they'd get nothing from him by making threats, he was an old man, he wasn't afraid of dying. One of them punched him on the chin; this didn't make him change his mind but it did leave him with a dislocated jaw, the effects of which he suffered for a long time after. To resolve the situation, Safouan came up with the idea of writing a cheque which enabled the attackers to beat a retreat without losing face.

Lacan told me of this incident in reply to my question about the knuckleduster he always carried with him. He'd armed himself with it after this attack. The weapon slipped into his trouser pocket to join his handkerchief, his bunch of keys, his little multi-blade tortoise-shell knife from Émile Peter's cutlery store in Paris, with its leather pouch, as well as a charming triangular boxwood netsuke, very smooth to the touch, that resembled a flattened Moebius strip.

Pierre Goldman too had planned to rob Lacan.[2] But he had been disarmed by the sight of the white-haired man walking down the stairs of 5 rue de Lille in Paris, completely absorbed in his thoughts. The thinker's austere and stately gait stopped him in his tracks. It relegated to the distant background Lacan's reputation as a celebrity, and his alleged wealth, a wealth that stoked criticism and envy.

The knuckleduster tended to cause problems when Lacan went through the metal detectors at

2 Translator's note: Goldman was a guerilla fighter and left-wing intellectual responsible for several robberies.

airports as it regularly set off the alarm. He had to empty his pockets. In those days, the weapon wasn't confiscated, but handed over to an air hostess for the duration of the flight, and restored to its owner upon landing.

While no prohibition, no conventional limit ever led him to stray from his course, he still recognized the real when it barred his path. He paid no attention to prohibitions; perhaps this is why he was in direct contact with what, over time, comprised his main object of study. The real was a serious matter; it was worth taking it fully into account. The real is what you can do nothing about, what you come up against; it is the insurmountable, that which is impossible to bypass or negotiate. In his case, in life as when he was treating a patient, the point was to get to that real, that indestructible kernel of reality; and anything that separates one from it, keeps it at bay or disguises it, is merely frivolous.

What was, for me, the first example of this attitude of his was the way he visited museums and churches in Italy. The opening times for these buildings are notoriously irregular and, what is worse, rarely respected. So Lacan didn't respect them, and endeavoured to have the doors unlocked, usually successfully. I don't know how he went about it, but if someone could be got hold of, he managed to persuade them. I learned that a closed door could be opened to anyone who asked with enough conviction. You had only to ask, and the door swung open as if by magic. As far as I can remember, there was only one time when things nearly ended badly; Lacan had aged, his stubbornness outweighed the flexibility of negotiation, he tried to push his way past, but the guardian, who was no respecter of age, shoved him back and almost sent him flying down the stairs.

The first church that I visited with him was Sant'Agostino in Rome, where Caravaggio's *Madonna of the Pilgrims* is held. Just this once, we found it open. Lacan gazed for a long time at the painting, placed above an altar. The Virgin's bare foot captivated him. He asked the sacristan who happened to be there to bring him a ladder for a closer look. The sacristan was at first reluctant, but eventually laughed and granted this unusual request. Lacan climbed up the ladder and scrutinized this foot in the greatest detail; it intrigued him for some reason that remained a mystery to me, since he gave no word of explanation.

In the Galleria Borghese, there's another Caravaggio on display, and Lacan lingered in front of this one, too; it has some similarities with the painting in Sant'Agostino. This is the *Madonna and Child with Saint Anne*. In both works, the Madonna is a powerful, dark-haired woman; the model for her was the painter's mistress, Lena. The Infant Jesus looks nothing like a babe in arms – he is too big and surely too heavy to be carried, even by a strong woman. The bent leg of the mother in the *Madonna of the Pilgrims* supports the child, preventing him from slipping down, while in the *Madonna and Child with Saint Anne* she is holding him under his armpits, as you do when teaching a child to take its first steps. In this latter painting, the Madonna's bare foot is crushing the head of a serpent, in illustration of the Biblical saying: 'And I will put enmity between thee and the woman.' The foot of the Infant Jesus rests on the Virgin's foot as if to support his mother's action. Lacan referred to this when he was giving a lecture in Geneva. 'The Virgin Mary has her foot on the serpent's head, meaning that she's supported by it', he declared. In both pictures, the beauty and the force of the Madonna's bare feet are striking. I wonder now whether Lacan, perched upon his ladder, might have been looking for a trace of the serpent under the foot of the *Madonna of the Pilgrims.*

That summer, Lacan opened my eyes to Rome and I fell in love with it. I'd already been there, but nobody had opened its doors as he did. Of course, we saw all the Caravaggios in Rome, those in San Luigi dei Francesi, those in the Piazza del Popolo, and his many paintings in all the museums, in particular the *Bacchus* in the Galleria Borghese and the *Penitent Magdalene* in the Doria Pamphilj Gallery, which at that time was almost always empty, and where the canvases were hung in the old style, one above the other, so as to cover the walls.

He seemed to know Rome like the back of his hand and he took me everywhere. In the morning, he would study an Italian guide book with a red cover, *Roma e Dintorni*, and choose the places we would be visiting that day. In each church, museum or monument, he would stop to look at just a few works which he gazed at for a long time, always in silence. It was only when I subsequently discovered his seminars that

I realized he commented, sometimes on several occasions, on this or that picture before which I had seen him linger. One example was Zucchi's *Amor and Psyche* in the Galleria Borghese. He also paid sustained attention to Domenichino's *Diana and Her Nymphs*, where you can make out Acteon hiding in the thickets, just before being transformed into a stag. The charm of the female figures, especially that of the two young girls in the foreground, lower left, makes the picture's atmosphere of cruel, impetuous energy all the more disturbing. The version of femininity that is intimated here tallied with Lacan's ideas on this question. The *Apollo and Daphne*, which represents another metamorphosis, also attracted his attention each time that we went to the Villa Borghese.

Lacan especially loved Bernini's works. He never wearied of contemplating the Fountain of the Four Rivers and its marvellous bestiary in the Piazza Navona, near the Hotel Raphael where he liked to stay. He returned to it constantly, in the way one returns to a source – it was the starting point and the destination of all our wanderings.

In the same way, we would spend hours amid the austere magnificence of the Palatine or the

Domus Aurea, which were as yet unspoiled by the restorations and the anachronistic illuminations. I also remember our visit to the basilica of San Clemente al Laterano, which contains within its depths another early Christian basilica and, beneath this, the remains of a temple dedicated to the cult of Mithras. These strata were reminiscent of the archaeological model of the unconscious in Freud's image.

Lacan also took me to more secret places, showing me, for instance, an anamorphosis well known to specialists in the convent of Santa Trinità dei Monti. This is a fresco by Emmanuel Maignan which, when you face it directly, shows Saint Francis of Paola; but if you move aside, a whole landscape appears in the folds of the saint's mantle: a tower, figures in a port, a boat.

This mural is located in a corridor of the convent that has housed the Sisters of the Society of the Sacred Heart ever since the disappearance of the order of Minims founded by Saint Francis of Paola. The members of this teaching community were not strictly enclosed. Lacan easily obtained the key giving access to the convent. In the evening, he took it from his pocket and showed it to me as a trophy. I don't quite know how, but he had managed to leave the building without handing the key back. He didn't like closed doors any more than he liked red traffic lights. Enclosure was a challenge he had accepted, maliciously suggesting that he could have violated the building's privacy under cover of night if he had wanted to. The next morning, he returned the key to the extern sister, who was discreetly amused by his little joke.

Lacan really liked Catholic Rome. As a result, we went to see a cardinal he knew, to whom he had entrusted a copy of his *Ecrits* to deliver to the pope. This man, a French member of the Curia, was served by sisters who opened the door to us and took us into his apartment. From its open window, you could hear the noises of the neighbourhood, the shouts of children and brief bursts of women chattering, all the hubbub of life that seemed to charm this prelate, not without a touch of nostalgia.

Lacan introduced me to a restaurant frequented by bishops and cardinals in cassocks, and run by one of the religious orders. This restaurant was called L'Eau Vive. It still exists today. Customers were served by young and rather attractive girls from Africa or Asia wearing their national costumes, as well as by European girls in vaguely Roman tunics. The atmosphere was discreetly erotic. I imagined that these young girls had once been prostitutes but had seen the error of their ways. The reality, as is often the case, is worse than any fantasy. I recently learned that they come from former colonies and are recruited while still very young by a community called the 'Missionary Family Donum Dei' affiliated to the Carmelite Order and including both religious and secular members. Though they do not take final vows, these girls, who are required to be virgins, are committed to leading a 'consecrated life', which means they have to observe celibacy and chastity but also, in between praying, they have to perform unpaid work in restaurant chains throughout the world under the name of Eau Vive ('living water'). There is a thin line in this case between religious life and slavery.

When John Paul II was Archbishop of Krakow, he frequented this restaurant whenever he was staying in Rome. When he became pope, he invited the young women working there to attend a special mass for them at the Vatican. I like to think that we unwittingly crossed paths with him (the dates coincide), in that place which had a certain charm, despite its ambiguity. At a certain time in the evening, in the middle of dinner, service stopped for prayer and hymns. Prelates, Christian Democrat politicians and diplomats at the Holy See rubbed shoulders or arranged to meet here, making this restaurant one of the most significant places in ecclesiastical high society. This amused Lacan as much as it did me, and we have often returned there over the years.

But his favourite Roman restaurant was the Ristorante Passetto near the Piazza Navona. This was the place in Rome where we first met up, or rather talked by phone. He was in Manarola at the time, while I was staying at my friend Paola Carola's on the Gianicolo. He had invited me to lunch at the Passetto where I was to await his phone call. He was known to everyone there and had an account at a time when credit cards were not current. This little detail always impressed me, as well as this long-distance conviviality he had managed to arrange.

I soon joined him in Manarola and when, a few days later, he went to the car park to pick up his car and head to Rome, I followed suit without even asking what his destination was. I would have followed him anywhere.

In Rome, we often saw Paola, who I had got to know in Paris a few months earlier. She welcomed Lacan with her usual grace and simplicity. Lacan's eruption into my life became a simple matter, too, an obvious fact, and it was one of the sources of my unfailing friendship for her.

She always remained associated with that summer of 1972, a magical summer for me. I discovered Rome and Lacan at the same time; I was constantly surprised by his freedom and his whimsicality, his indefatigable energy. He seemed to have that openness to everything which only belongs to young people, and the same insouciance. It was a moment of grace and innocence, the grace we need to open ourselves to chance, the grace that seemed to surround all those we met.

This was true of the beautiful and charming Jacqueline Risset, of whom Lacan was very fond; she had taken pains, that summer, to organize for him the showing of a film by Pabst, *Secrets of a Soul*, with a screenplay by Karl Abraham, a disciple of Freud. I remember one happy lunch, illuminated by Jacqueline's blonde hair.

It was another form of innocence that I discovered in Lacan's lack of prejudice in dealing with others: this made everyone feel freer. A whole set of potential obstacles to human relationships seemed to have been swept away by him. No doubt a certain psychoanalytic asceticism played a part in this, but it was also in his nature, that straightforward desire that gave him his zest for life and simplified everything.

Was it the same summer that he took me to visit Balthus at the Villa Medici, of which he was then the director? In any case, I remember the first time Balthus showed us the restorations of the villa on which he had been engaged for ten years. The kind of painting wiped or sponged over the walls was an original creation for which he was responsible, and it was amazingly appropriate to the premises, which emanated an atmosphere not unlike his paintings, especially in the apartment he had arranged. I fell under his charm, having already fallen for his work, in spite of the annoyance which his aristocratic pretensions inspired in me. At the villa, the employees called him 'Monsieur le Comte' at every turn. I could not help but think of his brother, Pierre Klossowski, who lived in a modest apartment in rue de la Glacière, Paris; Balthus made him look after their mother, Rilke's great love. Balthus invited us to take tea with him, a strange ceremony attended by prelates, assorted old countesses and France's ambassador to the Vatican.

Another time, we had been to visit him in the castle he had just acquired near Viterbo. Located above marble cliffs and dominating the country-side all around, the castle of Montecalvello was a mediaeval fortress so vast that it looked like a fortified village. Balthus had undertaken its res-toration, entrusting it to young trainees from the Villa Medici who could be seen, perched on lad-ders, busily working on the frescoes. The lunch was served by a valet de chambre in white gloves.

Lacan obviously liked him a great deal. Balthus was practically a member of his family, having been involved in a relationship with Laurence Bataille[3] for many years; he had met her at the age of sixteen, and painted several portraits of her. One of the most beautiful was at Guitrancourt.

Laurence told me that after the first sessions she had complained to her mother Sylvia and to her father-in-law that Balthus was being too

---

3 Translator's note: Laurence Bataille was the daughter of Lacan's wife Sylvia Bataille and her first husband Georges Bataille.

attentive. They had pooh-poohed her, and told her she should be glad that such a great artist as Balthus was prepared to paint her portrait. She didn't insist, and it was not long before she yielded to the great man, but she still felt bitter that she had not been given any support on that occasion.

We also visited Jacques Nobécourt, the Rome correspondent of the newspaper *Le Monde* who was married to a psychoanalyst of the École freud-ienne. He lived in an apartment whose windows opened onto the Piazza Navona, and which for me encapsulated, along with Paola's terrace on the Gianicolo, all the charms of Rome in summer. It was August, but the heat was not oppressive and the city without its cars was divinely peace-ful. Lacan seemed to feel completely at home, he knew all the museums, churches and foun-tains. We walked through the heart of the city, from the Piazza Navona to the Pantheon, or from the Piazza di Spagna to the Piazza del Popolo. I found the beauty of the place magical, I loved the sound of the fountains and the footsteps in deserted streets at night. I had fallen in love with Rome and this love lasted for a long time.

Love of food played a part in this. I discovered

Roman cuisine, both in the Passetto, my favourite, and in the neighbouring Maiella, frequented by politicians and journalists. We also often went to Sabatini, opposite the charming Basilica of Santa Maria in Trastevere, to Alfredo nella Scrofa, at the Quattro Fontane, and to Piperno's in the ghetto for its famous artichokes. Paola frequently accompanied us and also invited us to eat spaghetti on her terrace from which you could see all of Rome.

It was as if the summer would never end.

Once we were back in Paris, we became, so to speak, inseparable. But when I say 'we', I feel I am striking a false note. There was a 'he', Lacan, and there was an 'I', myself, who followed him: this did not make a 'we'. Moreover, if using the pronoun 'we' has never come altogether naturally to me, it was profoundly alien to Lacan. He could say that he was 'writhing at your feet', this wasn't completely false – it sometimes happened quite literally – but it had nothing to do with any 'us', of course. His profound solitude, his 'apartism' ruled out any 'we'. But that did not stop him from being what these days would in French be called *fusionnel*, that is, someone who constantly demanded your presence at his side. Even when at weekends he was preparing for his seminar, he shared his working space without difficulty; you could never get in his way as he was so concentrated on his work, and he loved to have you within reach. Besides, he did not like solitude, and was obviously not used to it. And later, when

I went away, I was afraid he might invite some new conquest to Guitrancourt. So I very rarely left the place.

In the early days, Lacan, who was a tease, told me that women always resemble some scourge or other. I myself, and my kind of woman, was like a flood. I secretly told myself that he did not put up any barrier against the Pacific surges of this invasion. And Gloria had not vetoed, as she had done for others, my presence at 5 rue de Lille. My youth, my discretion had disarmed her, and she adopted me. The only obstacle was T., who for ten years already had occupied an important place – albeit far from unique – in Lacan's life. To my great hurt, he spent most of his weekends in Guitrancourt with her. At first I tried to pay him back in his own coin, but he seemed so upset that I quickly renounced any spirit of retaliation.

He liked to claim that he was faithful. I had immediately realized in what sense this was to be understood: he stratified things. Refusing to let someone down, he never left a woman, even if, at times, he made her throw in the towel. He gladly remembered the women of his youth, but also the most recent ones. Thus he confessed to me that when we were in Rome he had stood up his last conquest, who was expecting him somewhere in Italy. She soon cried off. Having bumped into me in the rue de Lille, she sent Lacan a little message, which read: 'So that's the missing link between man and ape.' I had easily recognized myself, since I have long arms and a somewhat protruding jaw.

Since his first affair with a woman when he was seventeen, he told me that he had always gone for thirty-year-olds. He still hadn't passed his baccalaureate when he met a certain Marie-Thérèse to whom he dedicated his thesis in 1932, under the initials MTB. Their relationship extended throughout his medical studies. He proudly told me that Marie-Thérèse had paid a bookseller's bill for him when he was a young man, and she was the one who financed their holidays: in those days he didn't have two pennies to rub together. I was rather shocked, but also amused by this portrait of Lacan as a young gigolo.

He also told me about Olesia Sienkiewicz, the wife of Drieu La Rochelle, whom he had consoled after her husband's infidelity. He had clearly been extremely attracted to her. He enjoyed describing her typing his thesis in her underwear, in the apartment that Drieu had left for them. I remember that he saw her again and dined with her in 1977 or 1978. This was after a request by Dominique Desanti, who was then writing a biography of Drieu and could not get her to give him an interview. Lacan loved people to make an effort for him, but he was also capable of bending over backwards to do someone a favour, even to satisfy a mere whim. He had several times climbed the six flights of stairs to Olesia's flat, as she wasn't answering the phone. He eventually found her and invited her to dinner. But he realized they had nothing to say to each other: 'She's moved on from men', he told Dominique. She was living with a woman at the time.

When it came to Sylvia, who later became his wife, he told me an anecdote worthy of Casanova. She was supple and agile and would come to him in his room at night time, climbing the wall up to his first-floor window. This was at the very beginning of their relationship, when he was still living with his first wife, Marie-Louise. One day, I asked him why Sylvia had stopped working as an actress. He replied, after a few moments' reflection: 'Yes, of course, I could have been Monsieur Sylvia Bataille!' He greatly appreciated her wit. One day, at a congress, while they were at the hotel where the delegates were staying, Sylvia went out of the room. Returning a little later, she told him 'Professor So-and-So is here'. Lacan asked if she had met him. She replied that she had recognized his shoes put out for cleaning in the corridor.

I had been with Lacan for several years when, having seen us cross the courtyard of 5 rue de Lille from her window in the building opposite, Sylvia told Lacan that we had reminded her of Don Quixote and Sancho Panza. 'I'm Don Quixote?' he asked. 'Of course', she answered. This hurt me a bit, but it was an astute comment. I tagged along after this man as he marched straight ahead, driven by a desire whose strength never ceased to impress me.

Lacan was very generous with his women. And when he gave one a present, he did not forget the others. He covered them with jewels and foliage. It was his way of paying them homage, and this homage was long-lasting. Foliage plants flocked to my house. Some of them are still alive after forty years. When it came to jewellery, I was less keen. But Lacan encouraged me to over-come my reticence and all that belongs to the register of what I would call 'defensiveness'. The first time I met him, he saw me curled up in my armchair, wrapped in a shawl, and asked me why I was ensconced like that. I replied that I was 'shy'. 'What on earth does that mean?' he haughtily retorted. And the first time I came to Guitrancourt, he pointed out to me, this time with a smile, that I was 'wrapping myself up in my little shoes'.

Being defensive or off-handed, or making excuses, met with his disapproval. Usually he did not attack them head-on; he made a joke about them; that was enough. However, he was more direct when it came to his disciples, when he saw them getting tied up by their inhibitions or sticking obstinately to their excuses. He called on participants at his seminars and at congresses to cut to the chase, and was annoyed by their timidity. So if a woman was reading out her text, he would rebuke her: 'Do you think you might be brave enough to dive right in?', 'Say what you have to say ...'

In 1972, the light of the summer lasted well into autumn. It illuminated a new life. I accompanied Lacan everywhere. In Barcelona, where he was invited to give a lecture, he showed me round the Picasso Museum, which in those days attracted few visitors, and introduced me to the works of Gaudí and Catalan Romanesque art, especially the Romanesque chapels with their mural paintings depicting Christ in majesty in the centre of a mandorla. A young woman took us to visit the Abbey of Montserrat. Over lunch in the sunshine, she spoke at length about herself with an intelligence which pleased Lacan. He was very attentive, very interested, and showed a presence to the other that was one of his characteristics.

It was in fact one of his most striking features, this alternation between extreme attention, where he was entirely turned towards the other, and withdrawal, an equally complete absorption in his own thoughts. It could be said that presence and absence alternated in him, but absence is not the right word. When he was so concen-trated on his own reflections, the weight of his physical presence was all the more tangible; it was like having a rock at your side. If Lacan in motion, Lacan the ram, was impressive, Lacan when motionless was equally so. It was a total, unshakeable immobility, the reverse side of the decisive character of his relation to the world.

A few years ago, a young woman came to see me from Barcelona. She was writing a thesis on the history of Lacanian psychoanalysis in Spain, and knew that I had accompanied Lacan to that landmark conference which had not been recorded. I dug out for her the notes I had taken that evening. Scrawled in the margins there was a name and an address familiar to her. It was that of a well-known psychiatrist, a notorious Franco supporter. We had dined at his house, but I had no memory of it. She informed me that on the Internet one could find the extremely warm dedi-cation Lacan had written for him that day in a copy of his *Écrits*, as well as a letter which he sent him a little later. 'I was happy during this stay – and that it is thanks to you I have no doubt', he had written. I read this letter, if I may say so, with emotion, like a declaration that he had not made to me but addressed to another person, a declaration that had reached me thirty-five years later. A letter, he said, always reaches its destination.

For if he gave abundant signs of his desire, Lacan was hardly inclined to sentimental effusiveness. At the very most he mentioned Stendhal to me and assured me that he felt an *amour-goût* for me.[4] I rebelled against such a lukewarm attitude and demanded to be loved passionately. I would also say to him, with a certain malice, when he told me about his first women, that I wanted to be 'the last'.

That autumn, he began to perfect my education by getting me to read the humourists of the beginning of the century who had mocked the clichés of love. He told me about Cami, and in my library I found two volumes of his works: *Les Amants de l'Entre-Ciel* and *Christophe Colomb ou la Véritable Découverte de l'Amérique*. He liked to quote to me from the 'Album des Eugènes' in Jean Cocteau's *Potomak*, which he made me read. There are in it some nice sketches of the Mortimers 'who have but one dream and one

4 Translator's note: This is a calmer, more intellectual love than passionate love.

heart', a formula which greatly amused Lacan. The Mortimers are so united and so happy that they always seem to be asleep, unless their closed eyes are a prefiguration of their conjugal bliss. Lacan's love of *Potomak* was a reflection of his Dadaist side, which I think he never lost. He shared with the Dadaists their often caustic attitudes, their derision of the respectably conventional, and their taste for extravagance. He also liked to quote *La Famille Fenouillard* and *Le Sapeur Camember*. He particularly liked the famous adage: 'Once you've overstepped the mark, there are no more limits', which fitted him like a glove.

He also gave me as a present a more serious but equally humorous little book, a marvel of intelligence: Étienne Gilson's *L'École des Muses*. I thought, at the time, that this gift was a warning: I shouldn't take myself for a muse! But today I tend to think that he merely liked this work in which Gilson describes the avatars of courtly love in modern times, the dead ends and the misunderstandings encountered by Baudelaire, Wagner, Auguste Comte and Maeterlinck when they tried to update it to the style of the day.

He did not forget to supplement my education

in other fields, too. So, one day, I told him of a dream in which I lost my teeth, and I interpreted this as the expression of castration anxiety. He immediately told me to go to the dentist's, adding that if Ninon de Lenclos was still attractive at the age of seventy, this was because – and this was rare in those days – she still had all her own teeth.

Soon after Barcelona, Lacan delivered a lecture in Louvain which gave rise to the only recorded film of one of his public interventions. There was a crowd there, galvanized by the theatrical style which he deployed in response to big audiences. That evening, people saw Lacan the superstar. He spoke of death, which nobody believes in, he said, but which is the only thing that makes life bearable. Electrified by the atmosphere, a young man burst out and challenged him. The conference turned into a happening, though Lacan refused to back down, and tried to engage in dialogue with the troublemaker who, running short of arguments, ended up throwing a piece of bread soaked in water at Lacan's shirt. He was escorted out, and Lacan resumed his lecture.

The intensity of his expression, his dramatization, made me think of Antonin Artaud's

Theatre of Cruelty. Another evening in Paris, a few months previously, at the Chapelle de Sainte-Anne, he had proclaimed that he was speaking to the walls and this was exactly what gave his audience a certain *jouissance*. Theatricalization was part of Lacan's oratorical art. A mimicry of anger and ostentatious rage were its recurrent traits. They seemed to be aimed at his audience whose obtuse will to know nothing, whose deafness, in a word, doomed to failure his desire to be heard and understood. But if we gain satisfaction from being heard, we derive *jouissance* from talking to the walls. Beyond the address to an Other which does not hear anything, mainly because it does not exist, rage was aimed at the real. The real is when 'little pegs don't fit into little holes', he liked to say. This rage was something Lacan often expressed in everyday life, which gave him many opportunities to do so. On these occasions, his rage was not in the slightest theatrical and was generally not addressed to anybody, except the maliciousness of the real, so to speak. He got extremely impatient if he was forced to wait, even at a red light or a level crossing. If he was not served promptly in a restaurant, he soon obtained satisfaction by uttering a resounding cry or a sigh that resembled a cry. And if he went back to the same restaurant, he was sure of being served quickly.

This theatricality was reserved for an audience. It was an integral part of his teaching. It was a matter of using a mimicry of rage to communicate the intolerable which confronts the '*parlêtre*', being-as-speech, the intolerable with which the analyst must always deal in his or her practice. In private, Lacan was perfectly simple. Not in the sense of the great man whom we call 'simple' when he condescends to deal with his inferiors. It was just that, in his relations with others, he was deprived of the complications entailed by that dimension of intersubjectivity known as psychology. Lacan had no psychology; he had no ulterior motives; he did not try to second-guess the other. His simplicity was also due to the fact that he did not hesitate to ask for what he wanted in the most direct way.

My cousin Florence remembers having witnessed a disconcerting scene in Guitrancourt. Lacan had asked Jesus, the guardian, to procure a box of caviar from Petrossian, who for some reason or another had not managed to get hold of any. Lacan, unable to resign himself to the absence of caviar, began to implore Jesus to 'do something'. He could roar for what he wanted, even if it was the most futile thing in the world. And this was no theatrical display.

The day after the memorable conference in Louvain, Lacan recorded an interview for Belgian television, held a long discussion with the Belgian Psychoanalytical Society, and found the time to take me to visit the Musée des Beaux-Arts, where Ribera's *Apollo and Marsyas* made a great impression on me, as well as Brueghel the Elder's *The Fall of Icarus*. He also took me to the Béguinage, with its deliberate austerity that made me dreamy. A community of individualists – that is how I imagined the Beguines was just what I had always aspired to, I felt. Then he took me to Bruges. He made everything come alive.

At All Saints, we went to see Paola in Venice for a few days. We stayed at the hotel Europa whose rooms overlook the Salute, and we ate all our meals nearby at Harry's Bar, which Lacan liked to the exclusion of all other restaurants – so much so that the days when it was closed left him distraught. I kept, in memory of that time, a little message signed 'Dr Lacan', as he liked to designate himself, which he had written on a piece of the famous bar's headed notepaper and asked the waiter to pass to a nearby table where a couple had attracted our interest. He wanted to know which country the young blonde woman whom we had both been admiring came from. On the same piece of paper, the answer came back: she was the only blonde from Camargue, and her companion had chosen her to be his wife. Lacan was curious about everything and everybody, and always went straight to the point to satisfy his curiosity.

We went back together to Venice at least once a year. We stayed there for a week or two and visited the city from morning to evening; as in Rome, each time we would see the same places, as if we were dropping in on friends. Lacan always had his 'Lorenzetti' with him, the English guide book that is perhaps the most complete there is on Venice. Among the first things he had shown me, the most impressive were the Carpaccios in San Giorgio degli Schiavoni, especially *Saint Georges slaying the dragon*, with the dragon amid the heap of its dead victims whose shredded limbs lay scattered on the ground. In his seminar Lacan had mentioned this painting as illustrating the fantasy of the fragmented body.

In this painter's delicate works, calm and horror mingle. Another painting shows Saint George holding on a leash the dragon, dead or alive, which he has dragged to the feet of the king's daughter on the square of the city which he has just delivered. Another painting, where fear herself seems peaceful, represents the headlong flight of a group of young monks running away from a lion who is already following Saint Jerome like a dog. Carpaccio in Venice is rather like Caravaggio in Rome; you can go round the city, its museums and its churches, following the artist's trail, from the *Legend of Saint Ursula* in the Accademia to the *Courtesans* of the Correr Museum. But an even more productive trail is the work of Titian: his *Presentation of the Virgin in the Temple*, for example, echoed by the no less beautiful *Presentation* by Tintoretto in the Church of the Madonna dell'Orto, a little out of the way, close to Fondamenta Nuove. I loved that deserted area; we took the *motoscafo* to reach it, and not far from it, in the Gesuiti, is Titian's *Martyrdom of Saint Lawrence*, with its scene of night, gold and fire, which seems to prefigure Rembrandt. We did not fail to see them each time, nor Torcello, a place that Lacan was particularly fond of and not a great tourist attraction in those days. It was possible to admire at leisure the Byzantine mosaics of the cathedral, including the extraordinary *Last Judgment*, and to finish our stay with lunch in the gardens of the Locanda Cipriani.

In Paris, Lacan led a life of intense work. He saw patients from eight in the morning to eight at night, sometimes longer, taking an hour off for lunch, either at the '3', at Sylvia's, or opposite, at the restaurant La Calèche. I remember having lunch with him and his publisher at Seuil, François Wahl, as well as with his Japanese translator. At the end of one of these lunches, as we walked down the rue Jacob, François Wahl suggested that I use my influence to gently encourage Lacan to make some editorial decision or other, in his guise as director of the 'Champ freudien' collection. I was taken aback and tried to explain to him that I had no influence over Lacan and did not wish to have any. Apart from that, François Wahl was a man whose passion for his own profession made him a highly likeable figure.

In the evening, Lacan dined out, unless he was invited to the home of one of his daughters. He was a man of habit; he preferred to frequent the places he already knew and where he would not be kept waiting. Aside from La Calèche, which he liked because it was near, he often went to the Bistroquet, a restaurant on the Quai du Louvre run by a certain Albert. Serge Gainsbourg and Jane Birkin and their children went there, as they lived nearby. On the menu there were crayfish, which gave him the opportunity to make a slip of the tongue, a 'gender mistake', which he mentioned in his seminar as expressing his 'hysteria': 'Mademoiselle is "reduced" ['*réduit*', in the masculine] to eating crayfish', he had said to Albert. I loved crayfish but perhaps that night I was tired of them, and would have preferred something else. It was in this restaurant in 1976 that we had dinner with Philippe Sollers and Jacques Aubert. We talked about Aragon, who had grown old, and his relations with Elsa. Lacan had his own way of taking part in a conversation. If he did not ask a load of questions about a subject that intrigued him, he tended to be silent. Emerging from his silence, he intervened in an abrupt, often disconcerting sally. 'When a man is no longer a man, his wife squashes him', he had suddenly declared. 'Squashes him? Really?' I said, surprised. Sollers, on the other hand, had understood something quite different: 'When a woman is no longer a woman, she squashes her man.'

It was also at the Bistroquet that we dined with Jean-Jacques Schuhl and Barbet Schroeder in 1975 after seeing the latter's film *Maîtresse*. Lacan had stated that the film showed clearly that 'masochism was all put on'.

He also frequented Le Petit Zinc, at that time in the rue de Buci, where, one evening, we had dinner with Annette Giacometti. Its two other 'canteens', where we dined about once a week, were Taillevent and Le Vivarois, in the avenue Victor-Hugo. It was at Taillevent's that he had invited me to dinner for the first time, and I always enjoyed going back there. One evening, however, the waiters thought that Lacan wanted to leave and they rushed to pull the table away so as to free his seat, even though I hadn't yet finished eating. Subsequently, for a long time, until I made the connection, I was surprised to find I had no appetite whenever we went there. This has shed light on my childhood anorexia!

I went back there a few years ago. As I left, the manager came to say goodbye and I told him I had often been there before with 'Dr Lacan'. He remembered him very well, his silence and his heavy sighs. He had been head waiter at the time, he told me. He was quite moved by this memory.

My favourite was Le Vivarois, less stuffy than Taillevent, with simpler food, more traditionally French. The chef's name was Peyrot. He was a very nice man, and very taken by Lacan's odd behaviour, which amused him greatly. He always came over to chat with us, or rather with me, as chatter was not Lacan's forte. Over time, indeed, Lacan became increasingly silent and he would regularly take out of his pocket a sheet of paper folded into four, on which he scribbled Borromean knots throughout the dinner. I was not put off by this, and attempted to keep a conversation going by asking him questions to which he replied with a yes or a no. Most of the time it was a yes, as he agreed with the most contradictory statements I would make to test him out. One evening, Peyrot came over to us and said, 'Do you call that a dialogue?' This really made me laugh!

Peyrot was a little crazy. He would sometimes escape into the mountains for weeks on end, leaving his restaurant in the hands of his wife and his very reliable team, who adored him. All the same, his absences did cost him a Michelin star.

Some time ago, as I was leaving a restaurant that I had chosen because the chef was one of Peyrot's competitors, I told the manageress about the days when I used to go to Le Vivarois with Lacan. She laughingly replied that Peyrot often talked about him. He was convinced that the farts and burps which Lacan, as a free man, did not restrain in public, were meant to signal to Peyrot the two syllables of his name![5]

His busy working days meant that Lacan summoned people to him for those things which one usually goes out for. While he – inevitably – had to make an exception for the dentist, he would receive at home his hairdresser, his manicurist and his pedicurist, his gym teacher, his bookseller and even his tailor, who came twice a year with a bundle of samples of fabrics from which Lacan would choose the material for the suits and shirts which he had made to measure. Creed was a very old firm, founded at the end of the eighteenth century, which provided Queen Victoria and Empress Eugénie of France with their attire. It was a descendant of the Creed family, Olivier, who still ran the Paris firm, and who came in

[5] Translator's note: '*Pet*' in French is 'fart'; '*rot*' is 'burp'.

45

person to Lacan's apartments. The shirts he had made for himself were of great elegance. Because of these shirts, Lacan had abandoned the bow tie that he had worn for a long time. They had a straight collar, somewhat similar to the Mao shirts of the time, with the one difference that a tab with two buttons covered the two collars and fastened the shirt at the top. Lacan sometimes asked me for my opinion on the choice of fabrics: he often went for something quite sumptuous. His costumes combined a classic cut with whimsical, precious material. This gave a feminine touch to his way of dressing, which did not in the least detract from his manhood. His elegance was sovereign, not to say imperial; a little provocative and subversive. But, as Moustafa Safouan said, 'he played on his elegance all the more freely because it meant nothing to him.' It was an accessory, to put it mildly.

This splendour did not exclude asceticism – witness the apartment at 5 rue de Lille, which was almost entirely dedicated to patients, with the exception of Gloria's little office, a former kitchen that was now used just for breakfast, and Lacan's bedroom, also of reduced size, just like the bed and the bathroom. With no domestic staff, always eating out, at the age of over seventy he led the life of a student or a bachelor. I wasn't surprised by this at the time, as his way of life was similar to mine. On that score, we were the same age.

Shortly after Barcelona, Lacan resumed his seminars, which that year he called 'Encore'. It was one of his most inspired seminars. Throughout the year he talked about femininity, *jouissance*, the love relationship and the impossible relationship between the sexes. The Borromean knots, known as the 'string circles', now made an appearance and became increasingly important. Lacan had taken over this symbol of the alliance between the Borromeo family and two other families. Their alliance was represented by three rings knotted together in such a way that only one needed to be broken and the other two would be free. This knot really suited Lacan; it was a way of depicting the relationship between the categories of the symbolic, the imaginary and the real that formed the basis of his theory.

He also spoke of the mystics. It was not the first time he had mentioned them in his teaching, but on this occasion I may perhaps have played a part. Mysticism obsessed me and I had brought him the works of a Beguine (in fact, there were two of them), Hadewijch of Antwerp, in the hope that he would give me an interpretation of their inner experience. I got little in return for my pains. The way that he linked mysticism with feminine *jouissance* that year left me unenlightened. It was not the 'lusty fuckers', as he put it in reference to Teresa of Ávila, who interested me among the mystics, but those men and women (sometimes the same ones) who annihilated their selfhood. He said nothing about that, but in each session of his seminar that question, in which the enigma of my desire was at stake, held me in suspense. I was sure that he held the key to it and was simply waiting for the time to give it.

Perhaps each of his listeners was waiting in the same way. Lacan was a master of suspense. Each session of his seminar led to an abrupt conclusion with some striking formula that revived the enigma, announcing that the answer would be given in the next session – an answer that was always deferred. One of his students had formulated in a dream the impatience this stirred within him: 'Why can't he say the true about the true!' This did not prevent the feeling of a progress, an advance: on each occasion one could glimpse something new, as if in a flash of lightning that delivered an unprecedented (if only half-expressed) truth. This made his teaching resemble a spiral. We would go there week after week, waiting for a revelation which probably assumed, for each individual, the face of his or her desire. This expectation was always both disappointed and fulfilled by the unexpectedness of what he brought. 'Encore' was a good name for the desire that he never ceased to arouse through the enthusiasm that each of his witty sayings would stir. We were often stunned by his formulas, and repeated them to each other afterwards as if to extract the marrow from them.

Over the years, I didn't stop asking him about the mystics. One day I asked him about the psychic structure of Teresa of Ávila. He replied that it was 'a case of divine erotomania.' All the same, I finally wearied him with my insistent questions. At his seminar he eventually exclaimed: 'Mysticism is a scourge, as is proved by all those who fall prey to it …'. I stayed faithful to my question. I had to elucidate it for myself, over the course of several books.

The seminar *Encore*, published the following year, was the second to be transcribed by

Jacques-Alain Miller, just after the seminar on *The Four Fundamental Concepts of Psychoanalysis*, published at the beginning of 1973. Playing on my first name, Lacan dedicated it to me: 'To Catherine, my very pure.' He told me he'd thought of writing it in Greek, but had abandoned the idea when he remembered that I didn't know Greek.

Of all the dedications he made to me, my favourite is the one he used for his thesis and his first writings on paranoia, reissued in 1975: 'Gem Catherine – a Millot times better than these texts: give her in a knot what I myself couldn't turnip.' I suddenly heard the ambiguity thanks to which the Millot could believe herself a million times better, a claim well concealed by my modesty. I loved those 'turnips' among which the 'I' had dug itself, and also the homage of this gem, which made me think of the 'pebble laughing in the sun' which Lacan had on one occasion used as a metaphor for love.[6]

6 Translator's note: In French: '*Gemme* [which sounds the same as *j'aime*] *Catherine – Millot* [sounds rather like a conflation of '*mieux*', 'better', and 'million'] *que ces textes: lui donne en noeud ce que je navets pas* ['*navets*' means 'turnips' and sounds like '*je n'avais pas*', 'I didn't have']. I have highlighted the most

I also attended his presentation of patients in Sainte-Anne. Lacan was very keen on this exercise, which maintained his connection to psychiatric practice. For us, his spectators, it was an overwhelming experience each time. We witnessed an encounter, in the full meaning of the term, between Lacan and the patient. The dialogue would attain an intensity which testified to its decisive value for the patient. It seemed that his or her truth was coming into the witness box. It was also the figure of a destiny that took on shape and rose before our very eyes as doctor and patient spoke: the crisis that had led to the hospitalization of the patient conferred a tragic dimension on this destiny. Here, too, we were kept breathless, our hearts tense, caught up in this cathartic exchange.

We could also learn a great deal about Lacan's ethics and his practice as an analyst on these occasions. He never tried to beat about the bush when it came to the truth, and he did not let the patient slip away. He insisted on the points of the

essential puns in this knotty dedication. The French surrealist Paul Éluard defined love thus: '*L'amour est un caillou riant dans le soleil*'; Lacan quoted this in at least one seminar, and Millot here quotes Lacan.

real, on what acted as a buffer. Lacan confronted the patient by pointing out how reality gave the lie to his delirious psychic constructions. Thus, when talking to a transsexual who demanded to be treated as a woman, Lacan continued to insist that he was actually a man whether he wanted to be or not, and that no operation would ever turn him into a woman. And he ended up calling him 'old fellow'. This was a way of affirming his masculinity yet again while at the same time challenging him in an almost friendly fashion. For it was said without condescension, from that place where Lacan always addressed the other, the place of the human condition in which everyone is confronted with the impossible, our common destiny that often takes the guise of misfortune. This point where Lacan stood in his relation to the other was that of the irreducible solitude of each person, close to the place where existence borders on pain. It always brought you back to what, in solitude, reduces us to our exact equivalence with any other person, as Genet used to say. One day when I was telling him about what I felt was the rough deal of being a woman, he told me: 'You aren't the only one, it doesn't make you any the less alone.'

He didn't let his audience delude them-selves into thinking there was any hope for the therapeutic future of the patients. In the discussions which followed the presentation, after the patient's departure, Lacan did not hesitate to assert that one man was 'fucked'. He would even sometimes tell the patient this himself, which surprisingly had the effect of relieving the patient.

But if Lacan had a sense of tragedy, there was nothing theatrical in his presentations. He was just as simple with the patient as if he had been alone with him. This was in any case the feeling we had, as if we were witnessing their exchange without being there. However, he sometimes talked to the patient about the audience's presence in order to remove the embarrassment which the latter might feel. He used to say: 'They're all doctors', or sometimes 'They're all friends'! Or 'They're here as part of their education.' He would place himself in the position of someone waiting for an explanation from the patient, helping him to understand what was happening to him, in other words not knowing it in advance and wanting to derive this knowledge only from the patient. He would sometimes point out that he had received a certain specific piece of information from the medical team about the patient. He was always completely open about this, anxious to remove all consistency from the persecutory figure of an omniscient Other, possessing knowledge of the patient that the patient himself did not have. In itself, this position was a lesson about the use of transference in psychosis. But more than a technique, it was an ethics that he was conveying.

I wouldn't want to omit some account of how droll these presentations could be. The patients were often unwittingly comic, and this was also the case with Lacan. He was unaware of what everyone else knew: current words and phrases, the names of singers and sports personalities. He could question a patient about what a 'Formula One' might be with the same seriousness as if he had asked for clarification on some delirious construction.

Drollery, in fact, was a permanent feature of his behaviour. It stemmed from his sparkling wit, but also from his extravagance, something that was not in the least deliberate apart from the twisted cigar that was so emblematic of it – a baroque Punch Culebras which owed its twist to the braid from which it was extracted. Lacan had gone for this kind of cigar even before he grew interested in Borromean knots. His drollery was also due to his childish side. I often told him that he was five years old, the age of radiant intelligence in children (according to Freud), the age before the repressions that always afflict adults with a certain mental debility. Five years was also the age when, according to Lacan, he had cursed God. For me, there was not the shadow of a doubt that he had remained just the same. This idea did not meet with much of a reaction in him. Nonetheless, I once read somewhere that one day, over lunch, he had confided to his neighbour at table that he had a secret, and this secret was that he was five years old.

Thus, was I entirely drawn into his teaching. I devoted myself to it with passion and enthusiasm. My interest extended to the whole of psychoanalytic literature, beginning, of course, with Freud whom I had started reading a long time before. I was also curious about the history of the psychoanalytic movement, the origin of the splits which occurred three times during the fifties and sixties; Lacan had been the central figure in those splits, and his personality and his teaching seemed to have been the main issues in them.

The previous year, I had decided I might write

a thesis on this subject. Jean Laplanche had struck me as just the person to choose as a research supervisor, being at the time the only psychoanalyst who was a university professor. I asked him for an appointment which he granted me without difficulty. His waiting room was tiny. My evil spirit whispered that it had probably been set up in some old toilets. This cramped place contrasted with the vast office into which you were then ushered where Laplanche sat behind an immense table. The atmosphere was quite different from that of Lacan's cabinet. I told him about my project. He objected that the analysts who had taken part in this story would not agree to give me any information about it, that he was perfectly willing to supervise a similar thesis but only so long as I turned to England, where psychoanalysis had experienced institutional problems in the wake of the conflict between Melanie Klein and Anna Freud. He was even ready to locate funds to allow me to study the issue on the spot. The subject in France was obviously very fraught. Lacan, to whom I related this interview, immediately phoned Georges Balandier whom he knew well and who agreed at once to be my supervisor. Not being a psychoanalyst but a sociologist, the tensions in the psychoanalytic milieu were of no concern to him and, for my part, I was rather pleased by the idea of trying to approach the subject from an ethnological point of view.

I worked on it for two years, gave several presentations at Balandier's seminar, and discovered what I was looking for, that is, an ability to find my way around the issues at stake; but I finally abandoned the idea of writing my thesis on it. Laplanche had not been wrong. The archives were inaccessible, and the psychoanalysts whom I interviewed very reluctant to talk. The most comical, whom I will not name, was a woman who justified her refusal to talk to me by stating that either I was in analysis, and my research would only disrupt its course, or I was not, in which case I wouldn't understand a thing. So psychoanalysis really was an esoteric practice! But my desire to tackle this theme was probably premature. The 1963 split was only ten years old and memories were still raw. As for the split over the 'pass' in psychoanalysis, it went back barely four years.

Lacan, for his part, did answer my questions. He had even suggested that I go through the papers he had kept at home in a small box. These were not archives – they were in a state of the most complete chaos. And then, I was too embarrassed by what in my view would be an intrusion. I very soon dropped the idea. I still marvel at how, shortly after, Jacques-Alain Miller succeeded in putting enough order into this disordered heap to publish, in two volumes corresponding to the two splits of 1953 and 1963, documents, letters and circulars which shed considerable light on the course of events. One has to assume that he was less inhibited than me and surely better qualified. But I had been touched by Lacan's offer. He ignored the most usual sense of restraint and unassumingly showed great trust, together with a good dose of detachment.

During my work, I learned that Laplanche, whom I had consulted without knowing much about it, had played a role in the 1963 split, telling the IPA authorities that he had disowned the training he had received from Lacan, which had dealt the latter a severe blow. However, some time later – was it in 1974 or 1975? – Lacan went to a reception, which was quite rare because he didn't like such functions. There he had met Laplanche, and he came back really pleased to have seen him again. Laplanche had promised to send him a case of Pommard, the grand cru of which he was the owner. Seeing him looking so cheerful, I was astonished that he could draw a line under a nasty betrayal and I commented on it. In reply, he smiled from ear to ear. However, the case of Pommard never arrived.

At the beginning of 1973, Lacan wanted to go skiing in Tignes. I watched as he descended the slopes; I was as worried as the instructor who accompanied us, as Lacan's temerity was matched only by his lack of technique. I then went to Milan with him for a conference. On that occasion, he met the members of two groups, run by two of his Milanese students, as different from each other as it was possible to be: Contri and Verdiglione. One of these groups was called 'Communion and Liberation', a name which had the effect of exasperating Lacan who held the two terms to be the exact opposite of one another. The other group announced itself as 'Semiotics and Psychoanalysis'. A third group was coming into existence in Rome, at the initiative of Muriel Drazien, another of Lacan's pupils, probably the one closest to him; after practising in Strasbourg and Paris, she had just settled in Italy.

Subsequently, in 1973 and 1974, Lacan went to Rome and Milan several times to encourage his three pupils, his 'tripod', as he called it, to form a single group. That the interests of each group were obviously divergent did not discourage him in the least. He based his hope of bringing them together solely on the properties of the Borromean knot. Wasn't his 'bo knot' able to yoke together consistencies as heterogeneous as the real, the symbolic and the imaginary? It should therefore be possible to hold together, even if none of them wished to do so, a militant Catholic, a cultural agitator and a Jewish woman of American origin who was arguably the most authentically trained as an analyst.

During one of our stays in Milan, at a congress organized by Verdiglione, we had lunch with Umberto Eco, whom Lacan knew well, in a restaurant in the great Vittorio Emanuele gallery. He looked so happy to meet up with Eco again that you'd have thought he was a lover. Seeing him thus transfigured, I even felt a little pinch of jealousy. But there was nothing ambiguous in this relationship, Lacan just loved Eco.

On another occasion, when we were planning a trip to Milan, I had hoped, as it was spring, to stay in a country house. I had only to utter my wish and Lacan attempted to satisfy it.

Verdiglione endeavoured to procure us a house and a car with a driver. But as Lacan had a great number of meetings in Milan and I went with him, the comings and goings by car had made this arrangement very inconvenient. Lacan did not utter a word of reproach over what looked, with the benefit of hindsight, like a mere whim. I don't think he even spared it a thought.

During these repeated visits to the Italian 'tripod' which he was trying to set up, I witnessed the energy and the tenacity he devoted to this endeavour, one which failed, as might have been foreseen. He placed in the balance the whole weight of his desire, but did not take account of the psychology of each individual, did not bother with manoeuvring or winning them over to the cause one by one. In short, he was not a leader of men. All that interested him was testing the operative power of 'his' knot. His Don Quixote side was manifest here.

On only one other occasion did I see him dedicate himself with the same energy to institutional affairs, albeit in a different way. This was shortly afterwards, in the autumn of 1974, when he tried to support the reorganization of the Department of Psychoanalysis at Vincennes, as Jacques-Alain

Miller has suggested. He showed unequivocally that he supported this plan at meetings which were very stormy, as the quarrel was a bitter one. People shamelessly started to raise before him the prospect of his death. Lacan had to reply to one of his interlocutors who referred to his succession that he, the interlocutor, was not immortal either. He himself reported this piece of repartee back to me. During this period, I saw him enter into the melee, determined to prevail. I still hadn't joined the Department of Psychoanalysis and so I did not attend those meetings. I remember only that I realized that Lacan had on some occasion or another lied to his interlocutors, and I asked him why. He had not denied this and contented himself with a facetious smile. I picked up the message: he was not a man to prostrate himself before the truth.

Usually he didn't get involved in institutional politics and didn't discuss with anyone the problems that could arise in his École. For example, neither at weekends nor in the evenings did he ever make phone calls about the subject. Relying on what he had arranged, he was content to attend the meetings of the juries, of which he was a director, and spoke little at them. His relation to the exercise of power is one that I would describe as minimalist. His psychoanalytic practice and the seminar, in fact, kept him exclusively occupied.

In the spring of 1973, Lacan decided to visit Umbria. He had planned to go with T. He got me to agree that I would go with them. He was torn between his attachment to T. and his need for me, wanting neither to let the former down nor to manage without me, so he tried to solve the difficulty by bringing us together. As with his Italian tripod, it didn't work. I didn't have any fixed ideas about this kind of arrangement. Still, it would have taken a strong degree of liking for me to overcome that jealousy whose agonies I knew all too well. So when Lacan suggested that I go on another trip in July, also with T., I refused. I went to see my parents in Albania where my father had been appointed ambassador shortly before.

The separation was tough. Communications with Tirana were difficult. It was virtually impossible to phone. Letters took a week to arrive. Lacan had stayed in Paris, and wrote to me every day. Then he left for Lebanon and communications became even more difficult. Without any news of me, the tone of his letters grew harsher. 'I'm so angry', he wrote. Meanwhile, things weren't going all that well on my side. When I suffered an attack of tachycardia while swimming alone off the beach of Durrës, I thought I was going to drown. On my return to France, at the end of July, when I finally reached him by phone and he urged me to go and join him, I cracked, telling myself that the sufferings of cohabitation with T. couldn't be any worse than what I endured far away from him. I flew to Beirut. It was August, it was terribly hot; Lacan obviously bore the heat better than I did. The town was very modern, very luxurious. We were taken round by one of his students, Hadnan Houbbalah, who had recently settled as a psychoanalyst in Beirut, where he was to continue practising despite the bombings for many years.

Of Lebanon, I remember some very beautiful palaces, the ruins of Baalbek, and a lunch in the mountains where the mezzes were delicious. We soon left for Syria in the company of Hadnan Houbbalah and his wife. Near the border, the endless procession of military trucks suggested that war was imminent. We visited Damascus, Palmyra and Aleppo. I remember the huge, dark souk of Damascus, the beauty of Palmyra at sunset, and the pillar of Simeon Stylites, not far from Aleppo, which was not as high as I had imagined from Buñuel's film.

When we were back in Beirut, the French ambassador invited us all to stay in his residence, a palace in the middle of a park, a historical mansion called Résidence des Pins. In the evening we dined under the arcades in his company. But I lived this magnificent journey in a state of the greatest discomfort. The air conditioning added to my problems and I fell ill. This was the last attempt at cohabitation.

However, at the beginning of 1974, there was talk of a trip to China with Philippe Sollers, Julia Kristeva, Roland Barthes, François Wahl and Marcelin Pleynet. Lacan again suggested that I go with him and T., but I refused. Finally, he decided not to go, I never really found out why. Perhaps T. pulled out, or maybe she didn't get a visa? She did, however, go with him, in the autumn of 1975, for a conference tour of American universities.

Shortly after abandoning the idea of a trip to China, Lacan decided he wanted to go to Vincennes zoo to see the two pandas that China had given President Pompidou. This was not the only time we went. Lacan loved going to see the hippos, animals with which he felt an affinity, perhaps because of their shared art of yawning! These visits took place on Saturday mornings, when I also often accompanied him to see an exhibition.

In the autumn of 1973, the Congress of the École freudienne was held at La Grande-Motte, near Montpellier. This was a memorable meeting because, for once, a gale of enthusiasm swept through the interventions and debates. There was much talk about the 'pass', a ritual device which Lacan had invented six years previously, when it had led to a split, as I have mentioned. It involved gathering testimony from those who had decided to move from the analysand's position to the analyst's. Lacan wished to question the reason behind this passage, which, insofar as it marked a conclusive moment, raised the question of the end of the analysis.

This pass had left many analysts feeling baffled. But this time there was a feeling of a new path for investigation opening up, and everyone felt filled by a sense of renewal. Lacan's interventions at this congress counted for a great deal here. He compared the moment of the pass to the Heraclitean flash of lightning which reveals everything all around, as the crest of a mountainous massif suddenly stands out against the storm. He had got the idea partly from the seminar of Heidegger and Fink on Heraclitus, which had just been published. I had bought it and he had immediately seized on it, devouring it during the journey.

He repeatedly expressed the 'hope' that he placed in this experience of the pass. Usually, hope was not a feeling that exactly overwhelmed him. He had even said one day that hope led to suicide. What did he hope for? To shed light on the effects of an analysis, no doubt, as well as the nature of the analyst's desire ('whatever can be going through the head of someone who takes that step?' he would ask), but also to struggle against the weight of the establishment by appointing young and unknown people as 'Analysts of the École', which put them on the same level as the analyst trainers. When he declared, a few years later, that the pass was a failure, it was also the failure of his École which he was announcing. But that year, in Montpellier, the pass was very much alive. We had the feeling that we were participating in an exciting adventure, that of psychoanalysis itself. Lacan's desire dragged us all along in its wake.

During this congress, I had to face the challenge of 'coming out' about our relationship. I would have preferred to remain in the shadows, even in hiding, and I had taken a room in a small hotel far from the one where he was staying, with the notables of his École. But he wasn't having any of this, and I found myself having to cross the hotel lobby to the lift at his side, passing an entire learned assembly sipping their drinks and fixing us with their stares. I did not set foot in the little room I had booked. My concern for discretion was the least of his worries. A few years later, at another congress, he even had me paged!

From 1973–4 onwards, I accompanied Lacan to Guitrancourt more and more often, and soon every weekend. It was a beautiful house, an old eighteenth-century courthouse with pleasant proportions characteristic of that period with its taste for intimacy. It had been elegantly furnished by Sylvia. An annex had been transformed into a studio by a previous owner, a famous painter. It was here that Lacan worked in his office, facing the great bay window overlooking the garden. To the right of it, and echoing it, there hung a Monet, a Giverny landscape where the water lilies seemed to have been drowned under a cascade of foliage. When I settled down on a sofa opposite, I had it in front of my eyes when I was working there with Lacan. In the studio, a mezzanine had been created where you could contemplate *The Origin of the World*, concealed by a painting on wood by André Masson allusively portraying the very same subject it was supposed to hide. You could reveal the Courbet by removing one side of the frame and sliding away the Masson. Lacan took pleasure in this ritual unveiling. Pre-Columbian pottery adorned the edge of the mezzanine. I liked one of them in particular. It represented a woman's body with barely marked breasts, on the flared flank of which there clung a small being whose tiny proportions gave the mother a gigantic stature.

At a distance from the house and the studio, the garden had been enlarged on the right and a swimming pool installed, as well as a small house built on the edge. This included a room adorned with a Pompeian fresco which opened onto the pool through a bay window. Here Alicia, the caretaker, served the lunch she had prepared. There was also a small kitchen and a shower room, as well as a room arranged in Japanese style, in accordance with all the rules of the art, by an architect whom Lacan had employed on this task on his return from a journey to Japan. Every day, before lunch, in every season and whatever the weather, Lacan jumped naked into the swimming pool. He did two lengths, it was a ritual rather than an exercise, but it was still a discipline from which he never deviated. On the wall which ran alongside the pool there climbed various plants that bloomed in different seasons and were covered with all sorts of berries. Seeing their ever-changing foliage was a pleasure of which one never tired.

The pool and its house made our stays in Guitrancourt seem like real holidays. Indeed, we did spend some of the summer there. But it was also an intense place of work. Lacan set the tone, working all through the mornings and afternoons, in a quiet concentration. In the morning, he tended to stay in his bed. A small wooden drawing board served as his writing desk; the sheets of paper were held in place by a large clip. In addition to the night tables, two rectangular tables were arranged on each side of the bed, on which were piled books and papers. In the afternoon, he would settle down in the studio, sitting at the large trestle table facing the bay window. He remained there for hours, completely immobile apart from the movements of his hand on the page. This immobility impressed me very much, for it was totally unfamiliar to me: in comparison, everyone else seemed to be animated by a kind of Brownian motion. Together with his silence, this immobility formed as it were a central vacuum in the house, around which we would gravitate.

I am using the plural pronoun here, for his son-in-law, Jacques-Alain, and his daughter, Judith, and their children, came more and more often to spend the weekends in Guitrancourt, soon joined by Laurence and her three children. It was, for years, a family life with which I found myself associated. I watched the children grow up, we went riding together in the surroundings. They were good years. Lacan seemed happy to be surrounded by his family, even though he was often silent, absorbed in his thoughts. At table, for example, he did not join in the conversation much.

One thing I shared with Jacques-Alain was that we were both completely blown away by Lacan. This formed the basis of a mutual friendship. We also shared a love of badminton. Our game consisted of prolonging the exchange for as long as possible, and thus, contrary to the rules, making it easier for our partner to return the shuttlecock. This unusual way of playing favoured endurance and eliminated competitiveness. In the evening, in the lounge, where one wall was decorated with a Renoir, we sometimes played cards: neither poker nor bridge, but some children's game such as *barbu*. Lacan didn't join in. Apart from these games, and the time spent by the pool, especially on sunny days, we were all very studious. The many different places in the house meant that everyone could find the spot that suited him or her best, in complete independence: it was also a space of freedom. Conviviality and solitude were thus preserved and combined.

From autumn 1974 onwards, alongside Lacan in the studio, I did my work for Vincennes. I was investigating Freud's view of education, which became the subject of my thesis, and led me to re-read his complete works. From time to time, I would ask Lacan a question. Should I interrupt the course of his thoughts or wait for the right moment? He did not always reply. One day, I questioned him about the death drive and beyond the pleasure principle. Was a desire for death, I asked him, to be situated on the side of the desire to sleep or the desire to wake up? This was a question that interested him sufficiently for him to reply, after a long silence. This was a very circumstantial reply, and I took notes on it, which I kept as precious relics.

When I re-read them today, these notes, which were published in the journal *L'Âne*, seem to me to reflect faithfully the movement of his thought, his tumultuous character. He pushed on with his ideas until he came to a dead end and then went off along another path that also led to an obstacle; the whole thing circumscribed a zone in which thought is confronted with an impossible that forms a hole, or a siphon. In several of Freud's texts we find a comparable movement, repeatedly approaching the impasses by which the real is identified. It is something similar which we find in the progress of an analytical treatment.

That day, Lacan spoke of the 'dream of awakening'. Life, he said, is something quite impossible that can dream of an absolute awakening. I can now gauge how intensely this dream has long haunted me. He had added: 'This desire for awakening is none other than the dream of drowning in absolute knowledge, of which there is no trace.'

It was at Guitrancourt, during the holidays, that I wrote my thesis. It took me several years. The usual inhibition which accompanies this kind of exercise was exacerbated in me by a great anguish. I suffered a thousand deaths in the little green office of the main house, where I took myself off, alone and as if doing penance. I worked sitting at a table, which increased my torment due to a scoliosis that made this position very uncomfortable – and which I subsequently always avoided. In this small office there was a library that contained several treasures that Lacan had shown me, such as the limited edition of the childhood memories of Marie Bonaparte, as her analysis with Freud had enabled her to reconstitute them. On the wall were two early paintings by Giacometti: a self-portrait and a skull, acting as counterparts. Three French windows looked out onto the garden, but the room was somewhat darkened by the proximity of the trees. Such was the scene of my torture…

Guitrancourt was a convivial place. Lacan invited people to stay for the weekend, or longer, for the holidays – people whose work he was interested in or whom he liked. They included François Cheng, whom he had often asked, from 1969 onwards, to help him read this or that Chinese text. I remember that he had studied Chinese at the École des langues orientales, opposite his apartment block, during the war years. Over the course of these working sessions, Cheng was able to take stock of the concentration of thought that characterized Lacan, as well as his openness to the world, his incessant curiosity. 'I believe', he said in an interview, 'that from a certain period of his life onwards, Dr Lacan was pure thought. At the time I was working with him, I often wondered whether there was a single second in his daily life when he was not thinking of some serious theoretical problem.' Cheng recalled that he had brought their regular conversations to an end so that he could dedicate himself to his study *Chinese Poetic Writing*. Lacan understood this and accepted it with good grace, but not without heaving a sigh: 'Whatever is going to become of me?' This exclamation, this *cri du coeur*, was so typical of him!

After their last discussion, in Guitrancourt, in 1978 or 1979, when Cheng was leaving, Lacan said to him: 'Dear Cheng, from what I know about you, you have experienced, because of your exile, several breaks in your life: a break with your past, a break with your culture. You will be able, won't you, to transform these breaks into an active Median Void linking your present to your past, the West to the East?'

At the same time, Lacan often invited a mathematical logician, Georg Kreisel, who had been a pupil of Wittgenstein. A Jew of Austrian origin, he had been sent to study in England by his parents before the Anschluss. He had studied mathematics at Trinity College and had, after the war, specialized in the theory of demonstration. He stayed for quite long periods in Guitrancourt, in the summer. He had the beautiful head of an intellectual from *Mitteleuropa* and the air of an eccentric and somewhat hypochondriacal bachelor. Even on sunny days, he never went into the swimming pool. But he was far from being as eccentric as Lacan, who seemed to intrigue him greatly.

Was it in 1974 or 1975? I remember one weekend when there was a gathering of Jacques-Alain and Judith, François Regnault, Jacques-Alain's former fellow student and friend, Brigitte Jaques, Jean-Claude Milner, whose friendship with Jacques-Alain also dated back to their days at the Rue d'Ulm, Gérard Miller and Jocelyne Livi, as well as Benoît Jacquot, who had just produced *Télévision* with Lacan.

Until then, the latter had refused to appear on any televised interview, put off by the insistence and even arrogance of the presenters who had requested him to do so. Benoît Jacquot had come to see him, he was very young and completely unknown, 'a very little fellow', in the by no means pejorative judgement of Lacan who had been charmed and won over by him. The weekend was very cheerful. We played the society games that Jacques-Alain liked. His brother, Gerard, gave us lessons in hypnosis. Needless to say, Lacan did not participate.

When you see it now, *Télévision* creates a strange effect. To tell the truth, this was already so at the time. Anyone who speaks on television addresses the viewers as if they were familiar figures, in the intimacy of the same room. But Lacan seemed to be haranguing the crowds. He was addressing the thousands of people who make up the television audience. So he exaggerated the theatrical delivery of his remarks, all the more so since it was not a question of an improvisation, but of a text written in advance, in response to the questions addressed by Jacques-Alain.

Marc'O, a man of the theatre, who admired Lacan's style of delivery and often attended his seminars, was staying in a small mountain hotel when *Télévision* was broadcast. He asked the hoteliers to watch the broadcast on the hotel TV set. Everyone assembled at the appointed hour and carefully followed the film. At the end, the hotelier spoke: 'It's very interesting, very interesting. But where's the psychiatrist?'

Lacan continued to treat Benoît Jacquot with great affection. When the latter, shortly afterwards, brought out his first film, *L'Assassin musicien*, Lacan wrote a complimentary text in the *Nouvel Observateur*: 'His test piece is as distinguished as a master stroke. As a composition of music and images, I consider it, this film he has made, to be a masterpiece.'

He liked being surrounded by young people and was unstintingly supportive. This was the case with the first play directed by Brigitte Jaques, Wedekind's *Spring Awakening*, 'a tragedy of childhood' in its author's words, and one which had some similarities with Jacquot's film. I still remember the evening when we attended the 1974 Autumn Festival for the premiere of this play that seemed designed to attract Lacan's interest – he had written a short presentation for the programme. As in Jacquot's first film, it was moving to attend the debut of Brigitte Jaques, a stunningly attractive and very likeable woman, who went on to have a fine career as a director.

Lacan also liked to buy works by young artists who were still unknown, or almost. One example was François Rouan. Lacan had made his acquaintance at the Villa Medici and his canvases, made of woven thongs, reminded him of Borromean tresses and particularly interested him. He also accompanied me to the exhibitions of my friend Jean-Max Toubeau, from whom he purchased several drawings and commissioned a portrait of me.

That autumn, in September 1974, just before I began to teach at the Department of Psychoanalysis, I went with Lacan, Judith and Jacques-Alain and their children, as well as Gérard Miller and Jocelyne Livi, on a long holiday in Venice. In the course of this vacation, Livi took what are some of the finest photographs we have of Lacan. We see him striding down the quays, we sense his alertness of demeanour, his dynamism. He is elegant, he has a Punch Culebras between his lips, his 'Lorenzetti' in his hand. In other photos, he sits in the glass cabin of a *motoscafo*, with a smile and a sparkle in his eyes. Those Venetian holidays with his family were repeated over the following years. Laurence and her children soon started to come too. Lacan seemed happy with these breaks; he would drag everyone along with him in an intensive round of museum and church visits. His grandson Luc, who was five or six years old, kept up doughtily.

However, Lacan had just experienced a tragedy

from which he perhaps never fully recovered. In July, he decided to try and visit Albania; he was curious about this almost inaccessible country, a small enclave of Maoism under the grip of Enver Hoxha. My father had been posted there, so it was a good time to go. To get to Tirana, you had to travel via Rome or Budapest. Budapest had tempted Lacan; he was intrigued by this country which was going through the early stages of a process of liberalization, but he was also keen to know a city which had been one of the main sites of psychoanalysis in Freud's day. Sándor Ferenczi, one of his main disciples, had trained several analysts there, including Imre Hermann who still lived there and was more or less clandestinely practising psychoanalysis. Lacan wanted to meet him. He had been interested in the so-called 'clinging' drive or instinct. Jean-Jacques Gorog, a young Parisian psychoanalyst of Hungarian origin, who knew the language, accompanied us. For my part, I was going back to a place I knew: as a child, I had lived for three years in Budapest, where my father had been appointed an attaché at the embassy.

Budapest had changed. The first thing we visited was the Var, which had just been entirely restored. Another novelty was that you could now find shops selling household electrical goods and hi-fi equipment; they resembled warehouses. The women were often elegant. J.-J. Gorog reminded me recently that I had remarked on one of them in the street, wearing high-heeled shoes that I liked. I lusted after them and expressed a desire to find similar ones. At once Lacan began to run after the young woman and asked her where she had bought them. Gorog came to the rescue to act as an interpreter. The young woman said she had had them made after seeing a similar pair in *Elle*! Putting himself at the service of the desires of the other was part of the ethics of Lacan. For him, there were no small desires, the least wish was enough.

What had not changed was the political police. A relative of Imre Hermann, who drove us to his place, kept looking in his rear mirror, convinced that we were being followed. He had formerly been imprisoned for political reasons. Was it in the time of Rákosi or the repression that followed the insurrection of 1956? I don't remember. Lacan suddenly told him that it was surely the period of his life when he had felt the freest. I was shocked and wondered whether this idea had been inspired by Hermann in particular or whether it was a more general observation. That prison has the virtue of freeing a person inwardly is something that Arthur Koestler confirmed for me when I later read his work.

The great novelty was cultural openness. It was amazing for me to find, at a meeting organized for Lacan with students and teachers, that they were familiar with the works of French intellectuals such as Derrida, Deleuze, Foucault, Barthes, Sollers and Kristeva ... and Lacan too. In Hungary, as in France, this was a period of exceptional cultural efflorescence, which contrasted with the veiled terror which still reigned under János Kádár.

We were meant to spend three days in Budapest before leaving for Tirana. Lacan did not have the time to visit Albania. Two days after our arrival, he was told of the death of his eldest daughter, Caroline, who had been run over in Antibes. He was crushed, I saw him sobbing uncontrollably. He loved his daughter very much. He often dined at her home where he really enjoyed seeing his grandchildren. We immediately returned to Paris. Today, it is clear to me that there was for Lacan a period before, and a period after this bereavement. The general tenor of his mood changed. When I first met him, there was a gaiety in him that was part of his vitality. While this did not disappear altogether, his gaiety was shaken, he became darker in himself, more taciturn.

In the autumn of 1974, the congress of the École was held in Rome. It was organized by Muriel Drazien, the pupil of Lacan on whom he counted most for his Italian 'tripod'. She was assisted in this task by my friend Paola Carola, whom she had met on one of our Roman sojourns. She soon decided to come to Paris to train as a psychoanalyst with Lacan.

This congress was an anniversary; it marked ten years since the founding of his École. Moreover, in 1953, twenty-one years earlier, Lacan had inaugurated his teaching with his famous paper on the 'Function and Field of Speech and Language in Psychoanalysis'. This time, he gave a fine presentation, entitled 'The Third'. But he was not in the best of moods, viewing the large audience, as he often did, with disfavour, and (as he also often did) admonishing the psychoanalysts: 'Be more relaxed, more natural when you receive someone who comes to you asking for an analysis. Do not feel so compelled to put on airs and graces. Even as jesters, your existence is justified. Just watch my *Télévision*. I come across as a clown. Learn from this and don't imitate me.'

Jacques-Alain Miller echoed these words the next day, rather aggressively, simultaneously praising Lacan and lambasting the analysts whose fatuity he denounced ('what is fatuity? never wanting to prove oneself'), as well as their nihilism and their pretentiousness. Shortly afterwards, Daniel Sibony denounced in turn 'the noise of planks being nailed down and the pious claptrap' of this encomium to Lacan.

In short, serenity was in short supply at this occasion. It contrasted with the good humour and enthusiasm that had enlivened the congress at La Grande-Motte, a year before. There was a conflict brewing between the psychoanalysts of the École and Miller, whose theatre of operations would soon be Vincennes.

This was also a turning point in Lacan's relations with the École he had founded. The dissension that was coming to the surface would lead to the dissolution of the École six years later.

Lacan was unstinting in his support for Jacques-Alain. Thanks to the latter, the first volume of his seminar had just been published.

Until then, his pupils had discussed making summaries or rewrites of them that they intended to sign. Miller was the first to feel that it had become editorially possible to publish them in full. In the past, indeed, it was not customary to publish courses and connected material. He took the decision not to rewrite them but to publish a transcription of the shorthand accounts, the only traces of Lacan's oral teaching. This suited Lacan. In February 1973, the seminar on *The four fundamental concepts of psychoanalysis* came out. Two others, *Freud's technical writings*, the earliest seminar, and the last, most recent, *Encore*, came out in January 1975, a few months after the congress of Rome. The famous Bernini sculpture of the 'transverberation' or ecstasy of St Teresa of Ávila was the illustration on the cover. During the congress in Rome, we went back to see it in the Church of Santa Maria della Vittoria, together with Judith and Jacques-Alain, and the decision was taken with great enthusiasm.

That year, indeed, the enthusiasm was all focused on these questions: the publication of the seminars was a real event, and Lacan was also visibly counting on a new lease of life for the Department of Psychoanalysis. This was an experiment involving young people who were not yet analysts but mostly became analysts subsequently; for them, the teaching of psychoanalysis, its concepts, the texts that had marked the crucial stages of its history, was an adventure. I was part of it all and flung myself into it with all the studious ardour of which my youth was capable. Lacan, who had just before criticized 'academic discourse' and had viewed with suspicion the activities of Serge Leclaire in Vincennes in 1969, surprised the members of his École by this change of mind; it resembled a disavowal, as if he no longer believed in them to advance his teaching.

This did not prevent him from being fully involved in the discussions, during the 'Days' of discussion in spring 1975, when he often demonstrated his approval. Among his most enlightening interventions, I remember one in particular: 'The only thing that counts', he said, 'is not the particular, it's the singular. The basic rule means: it's worth crawling through a whole series of particulars so that something singular won't be left out ... If you do come across something that defines the singular, it is what I have nevertheless called by its name: a destiny.' He added that 'bringing out' the singular could only happen if you had a piece of good luck, and this could be seized only thanks to the rule of free association, insofar as it disturbs the principle of pleasure.

During the Christmas holidays, which we spent together at Guitrancourt, Jacques-Alain launched the idea of a journal whose title, 'Ornicar?', was selected during a game of portraits with Jean-Claude Milner and Alain Grosrichard. The first issue came out in January 1975, headed by a 'proposal' from Lacan called 'Perhaps at Vincennes ...'

At about the same time, I moved into an apartment in the rue de Tournon, a quarter of an hour's walk away from the rue de Lille. I went back there every morning, sometimes stopping to have a coffee with my friend Maurice Luciani, with whom I always had long conversations on love. In the evenings, I went by taxi to pick up Lacan so we could go to a restaurant.

It was no small matter to get a taxi at that time of the evening. I would sometimes be late and I would find Lacan hopping up and down and foaming at the mouth on the pavement of the rue de Lille. It was always an ordeal and one of the rare sources of tension in our relations, if I exclude the car journeys between Paris and Guitrancourt when he drove at breakneck speed – though I endured these quite stoically – and the occasional times when he was unfaithful to me.

I eventually realized that his infidelities occurred in July, as the holiday approached, when he had finished that year's seminar. On these occasions my anger erupted; he endured it patiently. His ability to endure feminine wrath was remarkable, and left me thinking that passivity, sometimes, is a sign of virility. For my part, I gave all the more free rein to my anger as I knew he would only ever do exactly as he pleased. Once July was over, I tended to calm down.

It was at the same time of the year that he wrote the texts he intended to publish. He let me read the various drafts. He wrote a first version, and once it was finished he binned it and began again, and so on. For 'L'étourdit', for example, there were three drafts. The first was the most understandable, each of the following two added a degree of 'complication', in the Leibnizian sense. He proceeded by condensations, over-determinations and equivocations. The text then had to be literally unfolded by the reader.

Once a week, I would cook dinner in the rue de Tournon, where he was often dropped off by his last patient. I was not very focused on house-hold chores, but he never suggested that he would have liked me to invite him more often.

Sometimes I would invite some friends to join him, especially my friend Marie Cabat, who lived with me in between her stays in Ibiza. He always gave them a warm welcome, taking a close interest in all their doings. For example, Marie played poker games at night and hoped to win often enough to support herself. Every evening, he would ask me how the previous night's game had gone. As poker turned out to be a bit hit-and-miss, Marie started looking for work. At once Lacan, always willing to render service, decided to send her to see the woman who ran the library of the École freudienne; he was quite prepared to impose this unexpected help on her. But the librarian was an institution all to herself and reigned over the premises of the École in the rue Claude-Bernard; she didn't see things the same way. And when Marie presented herself, she told him she could stay if 'Dr Lacan so wished', but that she had no work to give her. My friend beat a retreat. When I reported the interview to Lacan, he grumbled that she 'didn't want to work'. When I protested, he added, 'She doesn't want a career.' His formula suited Marie, who recognized herself in it. Moreover, in those happy days, 'wanting a career' was not an ideal. It would have been very inelegant to bother about it.

Lacan, who would go out of his way for you,

didn't take any account of the psychology of his interlocutors. So his interventions in your favour were not always crowned with success. A few years later, I decided to look for a part-time position as a psychotherapist in an institution. I had applied for one such job and I told Lacan, who immediately picked up his phone to support my application, presenting me as 'the daughter of our ambassador in Albania'. For him, this was clearly the best recommendation, and his intervention, as I later heard through the grapevine, had some success, but not in the sense that I needed…

I often talked to him about my friends and he always listened with a sympathetic ear. One of them, a psychologist, was unable to make up his mind and undertake the analysis that would have qualified him as a psychoanalyst. He said he hated the idea of 'paying the key rent'. I reported the phrase to Lacan; it had amused me, and he immediately rejoined: 'I'll give him a price that beats off all competition.' I made myself the messenger of this offer. Lacan kept his word. But it soon became clear that my friend did not want to pay the price, it wasn't a question of money. I don't know how he took leave of Lacan. It was probably not on the best of terms, for the latter told me to hand him a note he had scribbled on the table of the restaurant where we were having dinner and conscientiously stained it with red wine before putting it into an envelope, which he also smeared. I was not proud, this time, of being the messenger of this missive, a 'return to sender' for the way this friend had reacted to Lacan's generosity towards him.

Filled with curiosity as he was, he was very happy to be able to attend one of the experiments on elementary particles being run by my friend Lazare Goldzahl at Saclay. Goldzahl liked to demystify his research by introducing his visitors into the Holy of Holies of nuclear physics, which consisted of a kind of concrete casemate for sheltering you from radiation, with various computers placed on tables, in close proximity to the big particle accelerator. Lacan was attentive to proper names. In his seminar, he had commented on the name of my friend, which seems to refer to a golden number governing nature. Another time, having met Jacqueline Veiler, a friend of Maurice Luciani, a specialist in Quechua, he immediately asked him to introduce him to this language and took some lessons with her. At his seminar, he noted the homophony between her name, Veiler, and the French word 'vélaire' (velar), designating a consonant pronounced with the velum (soft palate). He thus brought out the way one's proper name can contribute to one's destiny.

In February 1975, Lacan was invited to lecture in London and Oxford. I could not go with him, as I didn't want to miss one of my classes, but I joined him the following day. Gloria had accompanied him on the trip and stayed with him until I arrived. He couldn't imagine travelling anywhere alone.

He gave a lecture at the French Institute, whose director knew him from a previous trip. He and his wife gave us the warmest of welcomes. She took me to Biba, a then very fashionable department store, and insisted that I buy two dresses, something I never normally did. I enjoyed wearing them for long afterwards, in memory of that happy stay.

Lacan then lectured at the Tavistock Clinic, a centre of psychoanalysis in London, attended by Masud Khan, whose works on perversion I had read, and who invited us to dinner at a restaurant. His *grand seigneur* style was a constant reminder of his princely origins. He was, however, very friendly; he was a brilliant man, a pupil and then colleague of Winnicott who had died some time earlier. At that time he seemed to have allowed himself to indulge in various transgressions that were frowned on by his colleagues. It is said that he ended his days in solitude and alcohol. The limits of his analysis with Winnicott were the subject of an interesting debate in the Anglo-Saxon psychoanalytical world, testifying to the freedom of spirit that reigns in Britain, even among psychoanalysts.

I have forgotten the name of the hotel where we stayed, but I haven't forgotten a teasing remark by Lacan, who had seen a portrait of Queen Elizabeth in the corridors and declared that I looked like her. For someone whose ideal beauty had been Brigitte Bardot, this was annoying, especially since it was not the first time people had told me this.

Some time later I accompanied Lacan on a visit to see Heidegger in Freiburg-im-Breisgau. Lacan had heard that Heidegger had suffered a stroke and wished, as he put it, to see him again before he died. He had known him for a long time, and had visited him first in the early fifties with Jean Beaufret, who had been Lacan's analysand. Lacan had translated 'Logos', one of Heidegger's texts, into French; it was published in the journal *La Psychanalyse*. In 1955, Heidegger had been invited by Beaufret and Maurice de Gandillac to a colloquy in Cerisy-la-Salle. On their way home, Heidegger and his wife had stopped at Guitrancourt where they had stayed a few days. Lacan had shown them round the region in his car, driving at breakneck speed as usual, in complete disregard of Frau Heidegger's cries of panic.

We flew to Basel, where we visited the excellent Museum of Fine Arts, before renting a car to go to Freiburg where we were expected.

The Heideggers lived in a newish house in a residential area, which hardly resembled the images of the cabin in the forest that I associated with the philosopher. No sooner had we entered than Frau Heidegger ordered us without further ado to use the slippers she reserved for visitors. I knew from my Jurassic origins that this was fairly common practice in mountainous regions because of the snow. In the Nordic countries, which I also knew, you take your shoes off when entering a house. But this was April, and I felt we were objects of suspicion as potential importers of dirt from the outside world. Freud had taught me that the outside, for the unconscious, is synonymous with the foreigner, in other words the enemy and more generally everything hateful. I was split between my unpleasant feeling of being an intruder and my hilarity at the unexpected contrast between slippers and metaphysics.

We were introduced to the living room where Heidegger was lying on a chaise longue. Lacan sat down next to him and immediately started telling him about his latest theoretical advances with Borromean knots, which he was discussing in his seminar. To illustrate his point, he took out of his pocket a sheet of paper folded into four, on which he drew a series of knots to show to Heidegger, who all this time said not a word and kept his eyes closed. I wondered if this was his way of expressing his lack of interest or whether it was due to the decline in his mental faculties. Lacan, who was not a man to give up, obstinately persisted and the situation threatened to drag on forever. Fortunately, Frau Heidegger came and ended the 'interview', at the end of a time measured in advance so as 'not to tire her husband'. We padded off to the exit in our slippers, having been invited to meet the couple a little later in a nearby restaurant.

I had definitely been irritated by the slippers,

and as soon as we had left the house I asked Lacan if Frau Heidegger had been a Nazi. 'Of course', he replied. At that time Heidegger's links with Nazism were not much discussed; the book by Victor Farias had not yet come out.

Over lunch, Heidegger proved to be somewhat more talkative, but the conversation was not very animated. Lacan could read German but barely spoke it and our hosts were not very good at French. Before we left, Heidegger gave me a photo of himself, in postcard format, on the back of which he wrote '*Zur Erinnerung an den Besuch in Freiburg im Bu. am 2. April 1975*', without any mention of my name. I was a little surprised at this autograph for a fan, a photograph that I hadn't asked for, but I preserved it piously. One of my patients, who saw the photo on one of my bookshelves, asked me if it was my grandfather.

Was it at Whitsuntide that year or the previous year that Lacan took me to visit one of his friends, Armand Petitjean, in the Cévennes? Petitjean lived on a large estate with his wife and nine-year-old daughter. He was very proud of the improvements he had made in breeding and agriculture, which allowed him to be self-sufficient.

He had been an ecologist from the outset and had found an ally in Edgar Morin.

While still a young man, he had made a name for himself as a young writer full of promise. At the age of twenty he had translated a poem by James Joyce, who had dubbed him one of the few people who knew how to read *Finnegans Wake*. He had been very close to Drieu La Rochelle, and initially made the same mistaken choices as Drieu during the war, publishing in the *Nouvelle revue française* which Drieu edited during the Occupation, as well as in some other collaborationist reviews, before joining General Giraud's resistance movement in 1942. At the Liberation, Aragon had demanded that he be shot. Jean Paulhan took up his defence. The fact that he had been a Giraudist rather than a Gaullist or a Communist was probably held against him more than an early support for Pétain that he soon renounced. He was eventually acquitted by the Comité d'Épuration, the committee that purged collaborators, but his literary career was destroyed by these events. The retired life he led on an estate over which he could reign supreme was his response to being cold-shouldered by history.

The bucolic atmosphere that permeated the

estate, and the discreetly patriarchal spirit of the host, now remind me somewhat of Adalbert Stifter's *Nachsommer* and the melancholy ambience of a place of retirement where everything had been patiently assembled, with refinement and simplicity, for the pleasure of the eyes and the taste. But there was also something desperate in the way such pains had been taken.

I kept from this stay a nice photo of Lacan leafing through a book with the daughter of the house, who had won his affection. Our hosts took us to the Nîmes festival where we attended a bullfight. Despite all the literary reasons I had to enjoy this show, I had actually been quite put off by it. While Lacan didn't share my dislike, he wasn't an enthusiastic spectator either.

Lacan was glad to reply to requests for help. Sometimes he was impelled by his liking for someone, as with Benoît Jacquot. This was also the case when Jacques Aubert came to ask him, via Maria Jolas, to open, in June 1975, the 5th Joyce Symposium that he was organizing at the Sorbonne. This was a real occasion, and for over a year fostered intense collaborations which led to longstanding friendships. As he recalled in his 'Overture', Lacan had met Joyce at Adrienne Monnier's bookshop when he was nineteen. The following year, in the same place, he attended the first historical reading of passages from *Ulysses* in French and English, shortly before it was published by Shakespeare and Company. So Joyce had been a longtime companion of his before Jacques Aubert came to see him; for instance, Lacan had quoted Joyce a few years before, in 'Lituraterre'.

In June, he decided to make this rediscovery the subject of his seminar at the beginning of the academic year, with the title 'Le sinthome', an old spelling of the word 'symptôme' ('symptom') which in French also sounds like 'le saint homme' ('the holy man'). Jacques Aubert spoke at length at this seminar, and one evening at the Hôtel-Dieu, in the presence of Lacan. This event was also attended by Philippe Sollers.

We became friends and have remained so ever since that summer evening when we met for dinner on the terrace of a restaurant facing the Pont Louis-Philippe – a happy memory for me. The exquisite kindness, the charm of Jacques Aubert and his wife Venette, who had come with him that evening, immediately conquered me, as they had conquered Lacan.

His kindness became real devotion throughout the year of that long seminar: Lacan was endlessly asking for his help, by mail, telegram and telephone. Aubert, who lived and taught in Lyon, often spent part of the week in Paris. If Lacan hadn't managed to contact him, he would wait for him in the evening outside his front door. He asked him, always as a matter of urgency, for bibliographical references and books on Joyce that he could not obtain, and wanted answers to all the questions that his reading raised.

In Guitrancourt, there were great piles of books, for example on the tables in the bedroom, and at least five or six lying open on Lacan's bed, as he read them all at the same time, jumping from one to the other. This was the first time that I saw him reading so effervescently. He worked through all of Joyce's works, in the original, of course, and all the commentators, mostly English. I became familiar with the names of Richard Ellmann, whom I read in my turn, Frank Budgen, Clive Hart and Robert M. Adams. The latter's work, *Surface and Symbol: the Consistency of James Joyce's 'Ulysses'* was a programme all by itself, just the kind of thing to keep Lacan interested, as he had long been captivated by the topology of surfaces and used the concept of consistency in connection with his Borromean knots.

He was so overwhelmed, so passionately immersed in these texts, that at times he seemed to be drowning in them. But from them he extracted, in his seminar, a bold but wonderfully simple new approach to clinical practice. Joyce's rigour suited his own. It helped him to re-examine the bases of psychoanalysis: what is a symptom, its relation to the unconscious, their connection with the categories he had long since identified, the symbolic, the imaginary and above all the real, which was increasingly the object of his investigations and, I would even say, the object of his torment.

During those years, his teaching became so stripped to the bone that it achieved an unprecedented clarity. He proceeded less than before in a logical way, relying more on dazzling utterances, striking statements that turned habitual ways of thinking, prejudices and commonplace assumptions upside down. At the same time, as part of this austerity, his style became less theatrical, and its aggressive edge had also been dulled. 'I'm getting older and nicer', he exclaimed one day. His kindness, together with his simplicity, was also what had struck Jacques Aubert throughout their relations.

Some time ago, at lunch, Aubert told me that, one day, Lacan had driven him back to the Gare de Lyon and left him there, saying he had a patient to see in his cabinet, but that he would return an hour later to say goodbye, before his train left. Jacques Aubert took the first train to leave, convinced that Lacan wasn't seriously intending to come back. When he got back home to Lyon, his wife told him that Lacan had called, frantic with worry: he had looked for him along the whole length of the train which Aubert was supposed to take, and was half dead with anxiety. So Lacan had indeed come back, as he had said he would. Aubert was sensitive to Lacan's behaviour, so surprising that it was in itself a whole lesson.

The year of Lacan's Joyce seminar, I managed to see, before it came out on general release, a film that made a great impression on me: Oshima's *In the Realm of the Senses*. I immediately told Lacan about it, and he expressed the desire to see it. I was acquainted with the producer, Anatole Dauman, and called to tell him of Lacan's wish. Delighted at this opportunity to get to know him, Dauman immediately organized a screening for him and suggested that he invite all those he wanted to come. That is how a certain number of members of his École found themselves watching it, somewhat to their consternation. Lacan mentioned the film at his seminar. He had been 'blown away' by it, he said, adding that it was 'feminine eroticism pushed to the extreme', an eroticism culminating in the fantasy of death and the castration of the man.

Dauman, delighted by Lacan, decided to invite him to dinner with actors or directors whom he thought might interest him. These included Isabelle Adjani and, on another occasion, Polanski, at the restaurant Lucas Carton, where I went to join them after my class at Vincennes. I arrived about half-past ten in the evening, dinner must have already been going on for some two hours, and Lacan was not very loquacious, as is well known. Polanski, accompanied by a young woman, wasn't very chatty either. Everyone seemed bored stiff waiting for me, and Lacan soon decided it was time to decamp. According to one of his letters, the dinner with Adjani, which I did not attend, wasn't any more enthralling.

In fact, Lacan was becoming more and more silent. He was absorbed in Joyce, and at least as much by his 'Bo knot', as he called it; the French terms *noeud bo* was a pun on Mount Nebo, from which Moses was shown the Promised Land and where he died. Ever since the seminar 'Encore', Borromean knots had assumed a greater and greater place in his teaching. In the seminar which followed 'The Sinthome', these knots took over almost entirely, in spite of the rather Joycean title 'L'insu que sait de l'Une-bévue s'aile à mourre', reminiscent of the translinguistic homophonic games in *Finnegans Wake* such as

'Who ails tongue coddeau, a space of dumbill-silly', in which Lacan, by his own admission, needed Aubert's help to hear the words '*où est ton cadeau, espèce d'imbécile?*' ('Where's your present, you nitwit?').

He did not just draw his Borromean knots. He also made them with 'bits of string' which he cut and joined end to end. I went regularly to the naval equipment section of the BHV department store in Paris to supply him with shipping ropes of the kind used for tapping and halyards, as these had proved to be the most appropriate for his manipulations. I bought them in different sizes and in as many different colours and braids as I could find. They needed to have a big enough diameter to splice them together with sticky paper. Usually, this is done with needle and thread, but Lacan couldn't handle a needle; he was far too impatient for that. A lot of research into different types of sellotape had been required too, in order to find the one best suited to this use.

Over time, the chains and knots started to take over completely. Lacan continued to manipulate them while listening to his patients, and the floor of his cabinet was strewn with them. Sometimes,

Gloria collected them in a plastic bag under his desk. They were also all over the place in his bedroom in Guitrancourt.

At the end of 1973, two young mathematicians keen on topology, Pierre Soury and Michel Thomé, had told him of their interest in his way of using the famous knot. This resulted in a sustained exchange which spilled over into a dialogue within the very framework of the seminar.

Lacan was forever asking them for help. As they did not have a phone, which was a rare commodity at that time in Paris, he sent them a great number of telegrams, a means of communication for which he had a great predilection. And sometimes he would go round and knock on their doors. He would have been so delighted when the mobile phone was invented! At that time, emergency pagers started to become common for doctors. Jacques-Alain joked that this was just what I needed to be equipped with, so that Lacan could reach me at any moment, just as he wanted. I had a lucky escape.

These telegrams can be read on the Internet; soon Lacan was sending them to Soury alone as Thomé had undoubtedly decided to cry off. His demands were always urgent, often formulated as cries for help, or even, literally, the word 'help'. Sometimes, at weekends, Lacan took Soury to Guitrancourt, where they spent long hours working together. At the beginning of 1978, unless it was 1979, when I went to spend a week at the home of my friend Marie in Ibiza, I learned by phone from Gloria that Lacan had had an accident on the way to Guitrancourt with Soury. He had missed a motorway exit and tried to turn off suddenly at the last minute, ending up entangled in the crash barrier. He came out unscathed, Soury had nothing more than a bump on the head, but the Mercedes, a fine white cabriolet, was a write-off. Lacan didn't buy a replacement car and stopped driving. The crash barrier was part of that real before which he bowed.

The pressure exerted by Lacan undoubtedly put a strain on Soury, but he was devastated when Lacan stopped his seminar and no longer needed his help. Knowing, however, that Lacan was ill, Soury wrote to him saying that he wished to undertake an analysis with him, but his letter remained unanswered. He was in a very bad state and wrote to his friends: 'I'm attempting suicide.' It was difficult to identify the body that was discovered on 2 July 1981, in a wood near

Ville-d'Avray. This was two months before Lacan's death.

In the last seminars, the exhibition of chains and knots increasingly took over from speech, which was often reduced to a commentary on the figures that Lacan traced in chalk on the blackboard. His remarks on psychoanalysis served as a preliminary to the knots that 'bothered' him relentlessly, over which he 'worried himself' constantly. It was rather as if he were seeking a way out of what kept gnawing at him in psychoanalysis, in the shape of that real that the knots now embodied. But is there any way out on the side of the real? That is to say, on the side of the impossible, as he had said himself?

At the 'Days' of discussion at his École, Lacan now made only rare contributions, often expressing his weariness, sometimes concluding the sessions with a simple phrase: 'It's gone on quite enough!'

I had even come to ask myself and ask him whether he was still actually interested in psychoanalysis, and even – a stupefying question that testified to my consternation – whether he had *ever* been interested in it. He immediately replied that it had been his passion. The word 'passion' was emphasized. In a way, this passion was still there, through his obsession with knots; a fascination that was more refined perhaps, and as it were radicalized. But he had lost interest in everything else, to such an extent that I quite forgot the ceaseless curiosity and gaiety he had shown in bygone years.

In the summer of 1978, we went to Sicily. He lost patience with everything; it was all too much of an effort. He had lost his enthusiasm for the visits he imposed on himself. One of his students, a psychoanalyst in Palermo, proved to be an incompetent guide, which increased his impatience. I remember feeling helpless in Noto, a city emptied by the heat, where we had got lost and could no longer find the monuments indicated by the guide books. In Palermo, he often stayed in his hotel room drawing his knots. I went out alone into the city and was assaulted. At the beginning of the trip, we had climbed to the summit of Etna. At the edge of the huge crater, among the gas and smoke, I suddenly became anxious, overwhelmed at the crazy idea that he might throw himself in, as Empedocles had done, and pull me with him.

This withdrawal, however, found its echo in me. I find it difficult today to resurrect the memory, as what was then rather akin to nihilism has become foreign to me. Yet if nihilism means the annihilation of all values, the term fitted neither him, devoured as he was by his passion for his knots, nor me, who set my commitment to psychoanalysis higher than anything else. I felt strangely in phase with him, as if I were rediscovering an old ideal in which everything could be reduced to its bare bones just as, for him, everything came down to his bits of string. Even before I met him, I was driven by a quest for the irreducible, for the one thing that would last, whatever it might be, and the determination to ignore everything else. This ideal, this quest came with a liking for the asceticism that Lacan embodied for me during these years of silence. All the vanities were consumed in his disdain for everything except the essential. Life with him was then like a great bonfire where all false values were burnt away.

So I seemed to commune with him, not in his passion for knots, which I had difficulty sharing, but in this lack of interest for everything that was not the sole object of his passion. In this passion was visible his unremitting concentration and his style which consisted in going straight ahead without consideration for anything but his goal; but it was a concentration that was even more refined, one that had created a vacuum around itself and could no longer change the object of its focus as before.

This attention to the irreducible in contempt of all else was something that I would put into practice in my relation with psychoanalysis. In all those years, my analysis with Lacan had continued. I had played for high stakes when I went to see him, and for me it was a question of life or death. We had embarked on the game and even if the deal had changed when our relationship became intimate, I had never even envisaged withdrawing my bet and taking my question elsewhere. Lacan had understood this; he took up the challenge and so did I.

I sometimes think that he had sometimes brought his liking for experimentation to our affair. He led things along, taking into account the particularity of the situation and making use of it when the opportunity arose. So he would sometimes suggest an interpretation based on some everyday gesture. Sometimes I told him of my anxieties about not being able to complete my analysis in such unusual conditions. One day, he replied, 'Yes, something is missing.' I was completely taken aback, since in my view there was something superfluous there! This missing thing, which sounded so definitive, fell on me like the blade of a guillotine.

Then came the moment when, in this work that I was still carrying out with him, a truth was revealed that plunged me into despair. Lacan could use a single sentence to preserve his trenchant tone and at the same time to temper its effects. This was the great therapeutic turning point in my analysis. The deep-seated anxiety that had gripped me all my life was lifted. There was no more iron hand gripping my plexus, no more fox gnawing away at my stomach, I gained a bodily peace that I had never known. Teaching and writing had been a torment; this also immediately ceased. It was as if I had become viable and life liveable.

The ground was cleared for a new and immediate desire to raise its head with all the force of an imperative: the question of having a child, a question that was all the more urgent because of my age. And it was too late to have a child with Lacan. This was a desire that analysis with him had freed from all its intensity, and I did not want it to remain a dead letter, for in my eyes this would have invalidated all the progress of my analysis. In the name of this desire, I cruelly separated from him so as to have a chance of fulfilling it. It was a wrench for me, and an earthquake for him.

Though I went to see him every day, and sometimes accompanied him to Guitrancourt, I no longer slept in the rue de Lille. Jacques-

Alain recounted how, one evening, Lacan slipped into the bed of his son Luc. The request was unmistakeable. Jacques-Alain and Judith moved to a new home so they could accommodate him.

Two painful years ensued. We had to go through the drama of the dissolution of the École freudienne, endure the violence that was unleashed and which did not spare him. I was left alone, too unhappy to meet anyone else, watching with growing grief as his health declined.

When he knew he had intestinal cancer, Lacan refused treatment. When Judith asked him why he had made such a decision, he said: 'Because that's how I want it.'

He was said to be afraid of operations. I never saw Lacan afraid of anything at all. It was part of his style not to wish to prolong his days.

At the last moment, however, he agreed to surgery. I was away from Paris but came back straightaway. He greeted me with a silent smile. In the hours after his operation, before he fell into a coma, I saw no sign of anxiety in him.

I returned to Guitrancourt a few weeks later. In the small green office, as I was heaving with sobs, I felt a black and bottomless hole opening up within me.

Today, I am the same age that Lacan was when I met him. Is this what made me decide to make these memories public? To honour our meeting, as it were, to be with him again … And I am also reaching the age when we wonder how much oil remains in the lamp, and everything reminds us that we must work while we have the light.

Memory is precarious, but writing resurrects the youthful freshness of memories. While writing, I have rediscovered many bygone days and, in sudden flashes of insight, the entirety of his being has been restored to me.